*Super
Smoothies!*

Candi Cole invites you to 'go beyond'
the protein-powder shake routine and the dairy-rich
smoothies of yesteryear. Her incredible four-season
collection of health drinks, is a rainbow of exotic colors,
whole food flavors and luscious textures that you won't
soon forget. Mother Nature's fruits, veggies, nuts,
seeds, grains and spices dance to Life in drinks that
promise to energize you!
"You have to taste to experience the orchards and
gardens in each luscious, nature-inspired recipe."
"Light and Clean" ... It's the New Smoothie Cuisine!

Also by Candia Lea Cole:

Gourmet Grains; Main Dishes Made of Nature
Not Milk ... NUTMILKS!

Revised and Enlarged

Super Smoothies!

Taste the Nectar of Life

FRUIT • VEGETABLE • NUT • SEED
GRAIN • HERB • SPICE
Enriched Blender Beverages!

By Candia Lea Cole

Woodbridge Press
Santa Barbara, California 93160

Revised and Enlarged Edition

Published and Distributed by
Woodbridge Press Publishing Company
Post Office Box 6189
Santa Barbara, California 93160
Copyright © 1996, 1993 by Candia Lea Cole

Printed in the United States of America

Distributed simultaneously in Canada

Library of Congress Cataloging-in-Publication Data

Cole, Candia Lea.
     Super smoothies! : taste the nectar of life : fruit, vegetable,
nut, seed, grain, herb, spice— enriched blender beverages!
 / by Candia Lea Cole. — Rev. and enl. ed.
          p.   cm.
     ISBN 0-88007-214-8 (alk. paper)
     1. Blenders (Cookery)   I. Title
TX840.B5C65   1996   96-7197
641.5'89--dc20   CIP

Cover design and illustration concepts:
   Candia Lea Cole
Cover art illustration and graphics:
   Michael Beery
Text illustrations:
   Kristine Lund
Photography:
   Tom Suttle

Dedication

To my mother, Barbara, whose own enlightened culinary instincts seemed destined to spark a lifetime of enthusiasm in me.

Acknowledgments

During the dawn of my life's journey onto a path of self-healing and the dusk which presided over my later work (writing books), many hours of seclusion took me out of the worldly arena of people and places while ushering me into the personal realm of exploration and creativity.

There were many angels who kept me company in spirit, as well as the angels who appeared by my side to offer their friendship and support!

I especially want to thank Thomas Suttle, my loving companion who, amidst the birthing process of three books, laid a foundation and shelter in which my creativity might flourish.

Michael Beery, who with passion and genius spilled colors from his paint brushes and palette onto my book's jacket, for a breathtaking gift to the senses!

Kristine Lund, a spirited and sensitive young woman, whose art career can't help but be aimed at the stars. Thank you for the gift of your illustrations that will delight so many.

Contents

List of Super Smoothies

About the Author

Candia Lea Cole has been creatively involved in food preparation since she began exploring the world of vegetarianism at the age of seventeen.

Candi became keenly interested in "diet reform" when, she says, "After a personal history of ill-health that was ineffectively medicated by prescription drugs, there was nowhere else to turn for help except back to nature."

Embarking on a whole-foods lifestyle, while learning about herbal medicine and holistic healing principles, finally paved the way to Candi's health and heightened spiritual consciousness.

Candi has since made it her livelihood to develop innovative ways (combining aesthetic, hygienic, ethical, humane, and economic principles) of nourishing the whole body with healing gourmet foods and herbs. Her recipes emphasize the personal and planetary values of preparing foods in a manner that honors creation (the life essence) while being kind to animals and considerate of our agricultural resources.

Candi's professional interests include teaching children, teens and adults the art and science of preparing health-enhancing cuisine, in addition to the principles of living in tune with nature. She has also managed catering services known as Gourmet Gatherings and Meals That Heal, and is currently a natural food product developer and consultant in Minnesota, where she lives.

Introduction

Recovering a Whole Planet

Dear friends,

Along the path of culinary ideas in this, my "third-born" wholefoods cookbook, I have scattered some of the tiny but precious seeds of wisdom I feel honored to have gathered from Mother Nature over the years of my journey toward wholeness. Sharing them with you is, I feel, both a privilege and a responsibility, as I am committed not only to my own health and wellness, but also to the progression of healing that the entire planet is now experiencing.

Like many of you, I share the urgent concern for the health of our environment and our children. The very elements that mankind needs for survival, including light, air, water and earth, are more threatened than ever before. Considering the fact that we unconsciously rely on these life-giving elements for the positive stimulation they bring our souls, it is no wonder that we feel bleak when threatened by their loss. Nature, after all, has always stood for good health and the divine essence of God, creativity and "miracles."

Although we have a lot of work ahead of us in order to change the conditions on the planet, perhaps the most important thing we can do is to stay "awake" and active in our quest for solutions. There are many blessings left in our lives, especially the original blessings of nature that can help us "remember" how to heal, and it seems meaningful to count them. The mystical glory of sunlight, for instance, still shines through the atmosphere even though the ozone layer is being depleted. There are cosmic, life-giving energies in the air we breathe even though it is more or less polluted. The streams from which water flows into our tap must be purified before we drink it, yes; but the water molecule itself is one of the most wondrous of gifts our bodies and the "body of the earth" utilize for sustenance and growth.

It's not arguable that much food production on the planet at this time is contributing to the destruction of rainforests and to the contamination of food itself (from pesticide fall-out to the waste products that are virtually synonymous with slaughterhouses). And, because our nation's topsoil is eroded, we can't deny that our food today contains only some 20 percent of the nutrients it did four decades ago! Nevertheless, each of us can pick up a shovel or hoe—and till our own organic roots and fruits.

We can join a community-supported farm where the biodiversity of plants and insects working in ecological harmony will lay the groundwork for replenished agricultural resources. We can say "no" to turning cows into perpetual milk-making machines—animals into our everyday dining pleasures.

To the extent that the problems of the world affect us adversely, we might each ask ourselves the question: "To what extent have I undermined my relationship with nature?" ("To what extent do I believe that nature is a separate entity from myself?"). As with any process of reconciling a damaged "relationship," we must be willing to understand what made us feel disconnected in the first place?

For the countless souls arriving on the planet each new day we must find a way to teach an appreciation for nature's "original" and sacred wholeness; showing how the power of nature, the "genius" of it, lives inside each of us. By helping our young ones cultivate a sense of our interconnectedness with all living things, they can begin to understand that we are governed by natural laws. They can then begin to think about the value of eating and preparing meals in harmony with the changing seasons of nature and be guided (even protected) by the cycles of life.

For those who are not taught to feel a personal and universal connection to the land and the forces of nature, it will be difficult to fathom how one affects the well-being of the other. They may never benefit from the realization that eating food which has no link to the land, no ties with the "sights and sounds" of "creation," cuts them off from the supply of wisdom contained in plants—the "real" ingredients for our wholeness. It is the deprivation of "real" food and real experiences around food (growing and preparing it) that causes so many to people nowadays to feel depleted in physical as well as mental and emotional energy. The makers of fast food and convenience foods as well as excessive food hype have stolen the healthy and primitive food instincts of many people, especially our teenagers who so desperately need to reclaim them.

Several things come to mind as I contemplate the will of both young and old to correct the false food habits and abusive methods of food production that have reached global proportions. First and foremost is the renewable commitment each of us must make to insure the higher evolution of ourselves, the planet and the human race. If you believe that nothing can be done in your lifetime to help the cause, do "something" anyway! As long as we inhabit the earth and progress along the "spiral" of life, the seeds of our actions and thoughts will matter. Going against the spiritual unfolding of our highest selves (a process which "happens" naturally if we are seeking growth) almost always brings undesirable consequences.

Personal responsibility is the premise upon which we can attain our commitment and the pathway that can foster our innate understanding of what it means to be well fed, as well as wholistically nourished.

In a very practical sense our bodies require whole foods such as fresh, organically-raised fruits, vegetables, nuts, seeds and grains. And until we restore our land to the nutrient-rich composition it had 50-100 years ago, we will need to rely on many of the recently rediscovered ancient foods and "super-foods" to nourish us. Many of these super-foods have been on the earth since time began but, because of the special places in which they grow, have not been readily recalled by the masses. In short, when we eat the natural foods whose content of nutrients and micronutrients are plentiful, we honor our bodies and the earth.

All in all, we stand to make significant progress in our lives when we realize that the 'true work' of our individual spirits lies in the act of strengthening and purifying the "body" so that it can perform the work it has chosen and create a better world in which to live. The inspiration for *Super Smoothies: Taste the Nectar of Life* as well the other books in my collection, with which I invite you to make an acquaintance (including: *Gourmet Grains: Main Dishes Made of Nature* and *Not Milk ... Nut Milks!*) was sparked by a personal need to strengthen and purify my body. The unique dietary needs I've come to know intimately have led me to explore wondrous new ways of my "adorning my fork" ... "filling my cup."

When you sip the recipes from this book, I hope you will think of all the sweet places that exude nature's essence. Then let the qualities of energy, purity and wholeness rebirth the miracle of life within you!

Looking to the light,
Candia

Part One

A Garden of Discoveries

Many moons have passed since a longtime pal of mine who founded one of Minnesota's most beloved health food stores asked me amidst a casual chat if I would consider "opening" her newly-installed juice bar.

As if it were just yesterday, I can recall my quietly surprised response as I sat envisioning a potpourri of soups, salads, fresh juices and "smoothies" prepared with down-home charisma.

Supposing that at least one of my eyebrows was quizzically arched, she jumped to propose a simple menu that echoed the murmuring going on in my head.

Her announcement that she had just ordered a fifty-pound bag of organic carrots for the upcoming days underscored her tone of urgency.

"I'd need you for just a couple of months—time enough to get apples and oranges rolling," she quipped.

As she schemed, I considered how the breezy sounding invitation might actually lead to a cooling down of fingers that had been confined to oven mitts all winter.

And I couldn't help but contemplate how it might bring a change of pace to the weighty culinary role in which I was seasoned to serve—caterer.

For at least a few steady years, my livelihood had evolved from my passion to celebrate food, nature, friends and the eating experience.

Getting into the spirit of my work usually entailed

fussing artistically over elaborate pans, bowls, and platters of eatables that would, along with flowers, stems and vines, produce an endless array of dressy buffet tables for many kinds of celebrations and occasions. Needless to say, such events were anything but hastily executed.

While comparing these past culinary visions to the carrot dangling in front of me (the juice bar), the novel impulse to support a fast 'n' natural bite to eat arose rather naturally.

Happily attuned, my friend and I shared in the task of readying her place for business only seventy-two hours later.

I shopped for an armful of appliances and potted plants, then hand lettered a wall-mounted menu while awaiting the green groceries that would lend a warm sensation to assuage hungry appetites.

As the days turned, I took to a barmaid's footsteps with relative ease, coursing to the beat of a bubbling crockpot one moment; the sizzle in a skillet the next.

Fresh vegetables initiated the industrious whine of a juicer which offered tastebuds a rich sip of nutrients. But it was the uptempo jazz of the electric blender that seemed to keep the "place" open to a daily dance, as arms flung across the counter for "smoothies to go" (from ten in the morn, 'til three in the afternoon).

I loved preparing the creamy blender drinks made from a sumptuous whirl of fresh-frozen strawberries, bananas, honey and of course yogurt or soymilk. Special extras sometimes included a hint of protein powder or a twist of peanut butter.

Those who hung close by and sipped the last drops through straws were an audible advertisement for the fast, easy, energizing recipe.

One of the perks of "chefing" them was that I could swig the leftovers at the end of each day. And I did, on numerous occasions.

The trouble with my indulgence was that I tried to ignore what I secretly knew were my food sensitivities—dairy products and sometimes, if eaten in excess, soy products.

Commercially prepared milk, with its hefty content of artificial hormones, drug residues, cholesterol and other undesirable factors, had been known to curdle my sinuses and upset my respiratory and digestive balance.

While yogurt (versus milk) was tolerable for me on occasion in an otherwise well-balanced diet, I found that the carefree consumption of it was enough to make me spend time clearing my throat of its mucous-producing tendency.

Following this dietary wake-up call, I decided to pay greater attention to my imagination of alternative refreshments. I also estimated how they might please the few others I had served who had similar dietary qualms and concerns.

Sometimes, when the juice bar closed at the end of the day, I found a spark of bold inspiration in the Tupperware container. Like a toddler tickled by a keen discovery, I was intrigued one day when I carved cooked orange squash segments (soup vittles) from the remnants of the green squash shell and pureed them in the blender with cinnamon-like spices, honey and water.

On another day, an equally delightful concoction was spun from an avocado half, tomato wedges, zesty herbs, a squirt of lemon, and liquid bouillon.

These drinks, I discovered, glided over my tastebuds in a uniquely delicious way and digested effortlessly—without the "moo."

"Squash Smoothies?" "Avocado Smoothies?" Something told me the general public wasn't going to relate to my new drink ideas just then—at least not on a moment's notice.

Well, perhaps I could have led their introduction with a rousing cheer. But with my spring-summer tenure at the juice bar nearly complete, and autumn inviting quiet serenity, I decided to bring my recipe sketches home with me, and use nature's longest upcoming days to refine them.

In my own kitchen, the freedom to develop and hone food ideas that were meaningful to me came naturally.

I found myself blending the colors, textures and fibers of nature in wholesome contrasts, in tempo with the ever-changing seasons in my mind.

Eventually these inspirations sought a place in my long-gathering culinary scrapbook wherein the seed ideas for maindishes, salads, desserts, snacks and so on had been flourishing for years.

Containing a garden of my most exciting discoveries about whole foods and the eating experience, I dreamed of one day sharing its abundance with people everywhere.

The idea of blender drinks is not a new one, nor is the idea of liquid nourishment. But what I hope you will find different about the ideas herein is the potential they have to lead your nose from the freezer and your fruit bowl (the places where smoothies are "thought" to originate) to the special places in nature, as well as to your body, mind and spirit—where a higher kind of culinary inspiration lies.

The wish to be satisfied is the desire of every man, woman and child. That "perfect balance" wherein the tastebuds are pleased and the body is neither artificially bulky and cumbersome nor frail and weak comes from a unique blending of the physical and spiritual life. When we can envision ourselves whole, as reflections of the greater whole, the conditions for creativity and healing develop in our soul. Then everything in our being reflects what we want and envision. And of course, the prospect for tasting something from our kitchen blender takes on a whole new meaning!

The real you, the essence of you, is like an emerging seed in the earth. When fed by the light and clean spirit of nature, it can't help but thrive!

'Light and Clean'

It's the New Smoothie Cuisine

I sometimes wonder whose imaginative wit dreamed up the name "Smoothie" to summarize the creamy, rich beverage that could have easily resembled malts and shakes in the generation before mine.

I enjoy the fun-flavored description. It stretches the potential of a blender drink to feature not only garden and orchard grown produce, but every fresh juice and animal-free fortifier under the sun as well.

For those of you who have parted ways with cholesterol-rich milk and ice cream drinks, and who may have also come to terms with food sensitivities borne of such, "Welcome to the crossroad for creativity!"

For others of you who are eager to explore your kitchen blender's capacity to become one of your favorite pieces of endurance-building equipment, I hope you feel free to shout "Bravo!" along with me.

We might very well agree that barbells have their place in life, yet maybe you've noticed as I have how they can muscle a wholistic perspective of nutrition away from even the best intentions for well-being. If you're one of the many individuals whose approach to making health gains has been to grimace and groan under the weight of iron and then gulp down "mega calories" every day, I'm trusting a book like mine will tempt you to take a breather.

Its "message" for pausing to taste and enjoy the "nectar of life," offers to lend you a subtler yet all-encompassing experience of energy.

Now before anyone gives voice to the mis-impression that my recipes are made to order for people whose career pursuits resemble Arnold Schwarzenegger's, let be clarify my true aims.

I believe that every adult, teen or child who lives an active life, exercising the muscles that shape their physique naturally, can be considered a body builder.

Hence, *Super Smoothies* is geared to the needs of every kind of body that is in the process of growing, flexing and doing aerobic activity. It is also aimed at bodies that are engaged from the inside, with "body-building" activities such as organ cleansing and healing.

As you explore the kinds of food-fuel to be gained from adding the enjoyment of my Super Smoothies to your health directives, you'll want to make note of one special thing. They aren't merely a frosty treat suited only to scorching summer days. Rather, they are a hearty collection of four-season beverages that the body can appreciate all year 'round.

On summer afternoons, when the appetite is stifled, chilled Smoothies provide healthy calories from which the body might otherwise be short-changed in the heat of the moment.

When chilly autumn mornings or snowy winter evenings arrive, enriched Smoothies can be served up hot in your favorite mug. They make better sense to the body's changing seasonal needs than puffed flakes, milk and coffee!

And if you're looking for something tasty to take

the place of pancakes, toast or eggs, they provide a wealth of protein, sans the additives of any special powders. Although we've all been accustomed to enriching blender drinks in such a fashion, it's really not a necessity.

An interesting article I encountered in a national health magazine recently brings this nutritional consideration into focus.

Director Wanda Koszewski of the undergraduate dietetics program at Cornell University was quoted in *East-West Natural Health* as saying, "The body is a well-organized machine. If you have too much of something, it throws the entire system off."

She was referring to the amount of protein required to build muscles and pointing at the likelihood that athletes may be unaware that an excess will hurt more than help their performance.

Relating the subject of protein powders, she concluded that "the only way those cans of protein punch will build muscle is if you're lugging them home from the store."

Surprised? I sure was. But not at "the fact" as much as the timely smack of her admission. As a vegetarian, I had long heard the news in this article—that plant foods contain all the essential vitamins, minerals, and amino acids (protein) needed to maintain a high level of health. Yet, there were enough occasions when having the belated truth in black-and-white print might have helped me win the debate with non-vegetarians.

Having a rather light and ethereal physique for as long as I can remember, moments sometimes arose when bulkier sorts offered to convince me that "bigger equaled better."

To "get there," I would only need to mix a few heaping scoops of champion weight-gainer powder into a liquid each morning, noon and eve and drink as they did.

Discouraged by the thought and deed of ingesting large daily doses of everything from dried egg and milk solids to soy, legume, peanut, whey and fruit pectin complexes, I stopped to ask myself a question: "Can my body, with its food sensitivities and animal-free preferences expect to utilize the benefits intended by a commercially formulated product? My soul answered, "No", adding that it would be much more content to build upon what it could see, smell and taste. Needless to say, the mystery of the benefits in the can containing a vanilla-white substance was left to the promoters and the can itself soon put back on the shelf.

This new turning point in my self allegiance led me to calculate which foods had the kind of proteins, carbohydrates and essential fats that would compete with or surpass a nutrient-dense protein powder.

Organic, dried and fresh fruits lead my exploration. Vegetables, nuts, seeds and even grains joined in, showing me that their textures and food nutriments were amenable to each other and to smoothie making.

The discovery of blending a combination of these ingredients with a variety of fresh juices, non-dairy milks, flavoring extracts and spices was a fun process spiced with challenge.

Nonetheless, "Butterscotch Yam," "Apricot Almond Orange," "Nutty Banana Amaranth" and "Raspberry Ruffle" found me tasting the rewards.

As I learned easy ways to incorporate these

nature-made drinks into my weekly dietary habits, I realized the enjoyable sense of stamina and vitality they gave me.

Finally, it mattered less to me that my flesh "should," by anyone's standards, bulge more, because I was nurturing an inner sense of being "light" in body, mind and spirit.

Almost everyone I know these days is opting for more lightness in their life. For most, this can't help but encompass the experience called eating.

We are all developing a greater sense of why it is important to avoid refined foods (including toxic chemicals and allergens) and animal cholesterol. They have the ability to congest organs, pollute the bloodstream, lower the body's overall immune function (causing fatigue)—and perpetuate global problems.*

While the goal of many of the fitness plans engaging the consciousness of people today is to become light and *lean*, I'm hoping many will expand their view to include light and *clean*.

The concept of clean eating is based on the increasing needs for our planet and ourselves to cleanse and renew.

Making a conscious effort to strengthen our relationship with nature and respect the life essence is a promising way to begin achieving this aim.

* *Pesticide & animal abuse, damaged eco-systems, etc.*

The deep voice of nature pulses through a fertile earth, then echoes in the sky; a harmonizing melody whose light and sound form the colorfully rich "tones" of a garden's chorus.

The Power
of Plant Foods

Warmed by Mother Nature's rays of sunshine and droplets of rain, the fruits of the earth are transformed by her life forces. It is these life forces that essentially offer to nourish, cleanse and renew our body's trillions of cells.

When the body's cells are enlivened by organic elements, wonderful changes begin to take place. One might discover the mind and brain becoming more alert as physical stamina increases. A gentle awakening of spirit may also occur, providing a subtle kind of nourishment (called inspiration) that goes beyond having food in the stomach.

Sometimes in our haste to appease the appetite, the flavors on our palates all but cause us to remember what food really is. Flavor, fiber, vitamins and minerals, yes; but I prefer to consider food also as containing the seeds of divine intelligence. To think that every bite of food we eat brings with it the energetic blueprint of a miracle, and one of which we are a part!

When we walk in a garden we can learn to sense this. Each and every plant, bud and flower offers to become part of us because we are part of creation, part of the miracle called life.

I know of no other experience quite like hiking outdoors to any flourishing field or garden and being drawn to something in a fragrant herb, sweet flower or vibrantly sculpted food; then, after taking it home to the kitchen, realizing that it offers a timely medicinal quality or health value as well as inspiration for a new recipe.

Nature is such a wonderful teacher as it nurtures our sense of who we are in relationship to the world around us. It can also stimulate reciprocal care in us as we learn to respect and care for the motherland as she has always intended to care for us.

From the standpoint of food and creative cuisine, I've always been more stimulated by plants than by animals. Plants are vibrant and varied, whereas animals, to me, have seemed relatively more bland, with a certain sameness of color and texture.

What gives me the most satisfaction in working with plant foods is my sense of being connected to their aliveness. It is unlike the culinary relationship to an animal whose individual consciousness is taken away at the processing plant.

Plants must also yield to the instruments of a farmer's harvest. Yet, do they not continue to pulsate with the sunlight that is stored in their cells as well as the vibrations of love and care that we (or others) transfer to them as they grow?

There is a sustainable life essence that we can tap into through our interdependence with nature. It is reflected in the goodness, light, color and the healing properties in every living plant.

Around the super-physical plane of our existence, you might imagine the invisible radiations of energy that invite this awareness.

The color wave lengths that constitute sunlight are an example. According to the scientific and spiritual findings of more than a few researchers on the subject, we can assimilate its energy vibrations through our diets by the process of metabolism.

Alex Jones, educator and author of the book, *Seven Mansions of Color*, explains: "As plants contain the sun's energy, they develop more of one particular color than others. In order to be healthy, we need to balance our diet so that we recieve all colors."

Jones offers one simple explanation of why so many people are overweight and undernourished: The body continues to crave food even after a meal because of color deficiencies!

The power of color to balance us has been proven by scientists as well. They have determined that vitamins are made of different colors.

Have you ever thought your body could be deficient in scarlet (vitamin E), yellow (vitamin A) or indigo (vitamin K)? With this compelling question, you might, as I do, find it very rewarding to devise colorful recipes that you might think of as a liquid form of light.

Because I've learned that the red, orange and yellow rays of light are stimulating and alkalinizing, I think of them when I've eaten more protein (acid-forming) than might be healthful. In such an instance, the body's internal balance can be adjusted by foods that range from fushcia beet and tomato red, to orange carrot and golden yellow squash.

Because green is considered a balancing color, symbolizing growth and healing, I try to eat some of it every day.

Although we recognize the vibrational color of certain foods due to the physical color we percieve through sight, Alex Jones qualifies that this is not always the case. Dark skinned prunes and figs for instance are said to contain the yellow energy.

Does this sound confusing? It is really quite simple.

In effect, we stimulate the whole body, its organs and glands, by assimilation of light into our diet, our eyes and our skin. Since light (color) is a vibration that seems to have an "intelligence" all it's own, we would do well to trust the way it nourishes all phases of our existence, including our mental and spiritual outlook.

It is the subtle elements in nature's plant foods that will empower us as we come to appreciate the power they behold!

Exploring the Nature and Art of Nourishment

If you are as enthusiastic as I am about reaping the color benefits of plant foods in your meals, I'm betting you'll also have fun imagining ways to mix and match their other nutritional qualities in Smoothies.

Often when I'm calculating what will go into a recipe, I feel as if I'm a "nutritional artist" at work. In fact, it wasn't long ago that I decided this description best suits what I consider my work with food to be.

When people sometimes ask me, "Can anyone become a nutritional artist?" I don't hesitate to answer, "Certainly!" And I encourage everyone to explore how the process for becoming one can greatly enrich their experience of food and nourishment.

Do you have a desire for complete personal fulfillment? Are you interested in "going beyond" mere culinary survival? (This frequently entails using your hands as food tools, versus the can opener.) If you answered, "Yes," you're ready to pick up a palette and create an expression with natures colors, textures and food fibers that reflects something

Cultivate the art of listening to your body, and create with nature's food the language of love that will nourish you.

meaningful about you and your unique nutritional needs.

Some of you will, I'm sure, estimate that you don't always have the time, finesse or domestic anchor to act in an artistic capacity with your groceries.

Yet I can assure you that these factors are less important to developing as an artist than is keeping a promise to yourself. The promise? To always explore your body's physical, mental, emotional and spiritual needs through a conscious awareness of what you eat.

Each day, whether you are dining at home, at a restaurant or at a friend's place, the ingredients upon your utensils are blending the quality of what you are becoming. They represent health and wholeness or just the opposite.

When in a state of disease or imbalance, it is not uncommon for most people to be drawn to fast foods and to bring chaotic or bland effort to meal preparation. The whole self's deeper needs for love and balanced nourishment go unmet. Although my Smoothies might be considered "fast foods" (because they are so easy to prepare), they encourage you to thoughtfully and artfully combine proteins, fibers, essential fats, carbohydrates, vitamis, minerals and amino acids for a personally healing influence.

Gaining an intuitive, if not intellectual, under-standing of how those food qualities appeal to you will guide your recipe art process. There is much useful awareness that Mother Nature will probably invite you to discover along your culinary way.

For instance, it is one thing to try to meet your dietary needs by eating a carrot while professing its vitamin A content. It is another, to sip the juice of it and experience its vital impact on your whole self. You might realize, as I have, that the orange color of this fresh-pressed vegetable is mentally and emotionally uplifting.

Or, that it is a friend to your physical body as the juice cleanses and detoxifies your liver and normalizes the bloodstream. In a spiritual sense, the "nature" of the carrot itself (a symbol of the creative life essence) might spark the divine creativity in you!

What an enlightening experience it can be when we realize that our food speaks to so many of our needs.

Tasting the Essence of Energy

Experiencing all of the abundant healing qualities in foods that correlate with their growth and fruition, is a wonderful way to realize what a friend and teacher we have in nature.

And learning to blend the individual benefits of foods into harmonious relationship with each other is possibly the most rewarding aspect of consciously creating wholistic health.

These days, whenever I set out to prepare a favorite recipe such as the "Gentle Fig and Mother Grain" Smoothie, I know that I'm also digging deep into the wisdom of its ingredients.

I'm not always fully aware of the reason why a food appeals to my culinary instincts one time and doesn't another. Or, why some food combinations seem to sing in unison while others savor "sharp" or "flat." But what I've learned is that whole foods promise a tremendous range of diversity.

The more we allow ourselves to "play" with them, and be open to a relationship with them, the greater our experience of wholeness will be. Let me share a personal insight with you that offers to convince you of this consideration.

When I first tied on an apron in anticipation of rendering a drinkable recipe *ala* the fig, it wasn't because I thought the meaty black fruit with seedy contents savored like "love at first bite."

Just as a ray of sunshine offers you warmth and security, may you know when it touches your lips that it is inviting you on a journey to higher culinary consciousness.

In reality I had never bothered to develop the healthy habit of snacking on this fruit's minerals or featuring it in popular holiday treats.

It was at my local food co-op that my lifelong perception of figs began to change, when I had the opportunity to sample a soft, golden-brown-skinned variety known as Calymirna. Then I began to fathom how it might mingle nicely with some other items I had alrready placed in my shopping basket.

Seeing how their pliable yet chewy texture would require softening in preparation for being smoothly blended, I hydrated some (in water from the stovetop) after returning home with them.

In a short while, I was humbled by the sight of what looked like blossoms, bursting with the essence of fertility.

A little bit of inspiration suddenly went a long way when I dropped them into my blender and watched them puree like a charm.

From there, I let the voice of intuition guide the juicy sweet pudding before me into a malt, as I drizzled in velvety nut butter, mellow brown rice syrup and a creamy hint of malted soymilk. Then came the instinct to fortify the blend with quinoa, the pseudo-cereal grain which botanists say is really a fruit. It was amazing to discover how this food could be transformed from its properly starched image on a dinner plate to a silky, concealed Smoothie ingredient.

After a few delightful sips, my tastebuds were recording their sense of all the romantic elements present at the orchards, gardens, fields and mountains where the seeds of its earthy yet elegant flavor originated.

Since developing this recipe, as well as others with similar appeal, I've become very enchanted by the idea of journeying to the global places my food choices flourish in.

For it's evident to me that they contribute to the essence of what a food eventually becomes and to what we become when we eat it. Take quinoa, for instance. This Smoothie ingredient is derived from a three to six-foot-tall plant whose stems yield large clusters of tiny seeds which thrive upon the high plains of the Andes Mountains in South America (as well as the Colorado Rockies).

I am impressed by the hardy and rugged mental view of them soaking up ultraviolet nourishment at freezing cold temperatures. Yet, to see how the harvest prefers to be cooked over a gentle flame as it emerges into near-translucent spirals of fluff, reveals a refined aspect of its whole.

I accept these qualities as the wisdom a plant brings me and rely on its symbolism to bring my body both endurance and refinement.

To study the scientific nutritional profile of quinoa is to offer the left side of my brain proof of its balanced protein content, minerals and easy digestibility.

Perhaps the only mystique remaining about a Smoothie containing this and other uncommonly good ingredients from nature, lies in the soft appeal of its name.

If you happen to be of the mind that a beverage named "Energy Blast" or "Power Lifter" would faster respond to your craving for muscle fuel, let me assure you of something honest. Your cup will always run over with true dynamism when you pour the essence of real energy into it.

No matter what name I find myself christening a recipe with, I want it to manifest the blessing of energy, the kind of energy that transforms the elements of light, hydrogen, oxygen, nitrogen and water within the tissues and cells of a plant to develop its color, fiber, shape, flavor and healing values.

Plants share in this all-encompassing source of power as they establish their roots in the world, and blossom in relationship to our bodies' changing needs.

They do this so that we may know the honor of our interconnectedness with a greater whole, and share the strength we derive from it.

When the health of your being is very important to you, that doesn't necessarily mean you give it the most time, but rather that your devotion to its unfolding in your life.

Get Ready, Get Set,
You've Got It Made!

When the moment comes for gathering up the bounty that will satisfy your body's cravings for food and your soul's urge for nourishment, you'll want to have your culinary corners decked with life!

So, go ahead and fill colorful ceramic bowls with the fresh fruits of the season. Give floor space to a big decorative basket that billows with squashes and yams. Stock a pantry with small bunches of grain and food fortifiers.

Keep a lazy suzan rolling with wholesome sweeteners. Perch flavoring essences, herbs and spices upon an easy-to-reach rack.

Tuck peeled bananas in the freezer, along with summer's berries. Spare a shelf in the refrigerator for jars of dried fruits and nuts, and keep a crisper supplied with vegetables.

Smoothies are so exciting to make when you have the inspiration for them around you.

Granted, the preparation of my recipes lends itself to more ingenuity than a "grand slam" of juice concentrate spun with instant powder. Yet, I invite you to see how a group of culinary helpers can make your moments in the kitchen worth your while.

Some of you may be tentative when you envision how appliances such as a blender, a nut grinder, a juicer, and perhaps your oven or stovetop can translate into a no-fuss recipe process.

You can relax assured, however, that these small electrics are not needed all at once to create a single recipe. Having them on standby will simply give you a confident sense of resourcefulness as you consider your options.

Of the dozens of beverages that await your experimentation, most call for a tidy composite of ingredients and a minimum of manipulation before they're ready to sip. "Chocolate Silk" and "Carob Sesame" sweet potato Smoothies are good examples.

First, the orange tubers (the sweet potatoes!) are baked in the oven or microwave. This step can be done in advance, perhaps at the same time you have the oven turned on for a dinner or dessert bake.

Next, the potato skins are peeled away from their tender flesh and can be sliced directly into the blender. You can then add such "yummies" as sweet carob powder, calcium-rich sesame tahini, pure maple syrup, vanilla extract and water.

The enriched consistency of this Smoothie (made in only minutes) is dark and creamy with a pudding-like quality that kids can't resist spooning from a dessert cup.

Adults or teenagers engaged in heavy muscular work (or workouts) will also thrive on this delicious source of carbohydrates and beta carotene. I particularly enjoy the fact that it is easy to digest (and offers to nourish the spleen and pancreas).

The easy appeal of the drink just described could be attributed to many of my fruit-based Smoothies as well. "Frosty Banana Elm and Currant" is one flavor that comes to mind.

First, it requires you to peel and freeze some ripe bananas in advance. Once they are hardened by frost, you can break them into smallish chunks in the blender. Then simply add water or any desirable milk alternative to yield its irresistible ice cream-like nap and flavor.

To give the recipe nutritional "character," I add a delicate blend of fresh walnut or flaxseed meal and juicy currants.

This flavor combo demonstrates a case in which an electric mini-grinder (such as a coffee grinding unit) can be used to pulverize nuts in only a few seconds.

If you like the idea of adding currants (they're zesty, sweet and mineral rich) you can reconstitute them, for a full-bodied flavor. As a time-saver, prefill small jars with dried apples, dates and raisins, then marinate them in water or apple juice. Stored in the refrigerator, they provide ready-made variety for an up to a week-long spree of drinking.

Just in case you're curious about where the middle name (elm) comes from in my "Frosty Banana Currant" drink, it is a fluffy beige, aromatic powder that's derived from the healing inner bark of an elm tree. Said to be as nutritious as oatmeal, I consider it as an ideal herbal body-building ingredient for vegetarians.

Another of my personal favorites for creating body-building recipes is to blend into them a few tablespoons of cooked grain. I often reach into my refrigerator for a pot of yesterday's leftover barley, amaranth, quinoa, teff or short-grain sweet rice. They complement recipes featuring sweet fibrous fruits such as raisins, dates, figs, prunes, etc. (see section on fruits).

With these few ideas, I hope you are gaining a visual sense of just how uncomplicated it can be to achieve marvelous new taste sensations.

Part Two

Harvest of the Bounty

A view of the many fruits, nuts, seeds, vegetables, grains and nutriments that characterize a Smoothie's nourishing potential.

Fresh Fruit

Without fruit, the refreshing appeal of a Smoothie might never have been conceived. There are so many qualities of fruit that make it fun to eat and drink. It is colorful, uniquely shaped, light and juicy, soft yet fibrous, low in calories and abundant in vitamins and minerals.

For many people there is something wonderfully sensuous about fruit, which is actually the ripened ovary within a flower's female tissue.

Practically all kinds of fruit contain 80-95 percent water, which is what keeps their calorie content so low and their recipe for sweetness (fructose, glucose and sucrose) light.

Fiber and pectin are the other benefits that fruits provide. Insoluble fiber such as the chewy skin of an apple or raisin coaxes the intestines into activity. Pectin, the ingredient found in the flesh and pulp of a fruit, can help lower cholesterol and stabilize blood sugar.

With the exception of avocados, fruits are virtually free of fat, and cholesterol as well.

The minerals we can expect to get from fruit include iron and potassium. Berries and dried fruits are considered good blood-builders, while oranges, bananas and pears are known to balance the fluid in the body's tissues.

Of course, the nutrients that fruit boasts of most include vitamins C and A. Citrus fruits and berries are the juicy morsels that Linus Pauling would have us love, as they are rich in vitamin C.

Orange and yellow fruits contain beta carotene, a potent substance which converts to Vitamin A in the body and has the potential to protect against cancer (because it is an antioxidant).

I rely on organically raised fruits for recipes whenever I can, because the waxes, pesticides and chemicals found in commercially raised produce pose a sizable health threat to the body. Our immune systems, as well as our body's filtration system (the liver), are more susceptible to being burdened by these elements than we realize.

For this and other reasons, it is especially important to wash fruit before eating it. I keep a scrub brush handy for the robust fruits and a bottle of gentle bactericide that can be diluted in a soak basin for the more tender fruits. Simply rinse the fruits under cool, running water after these measures are taken.

There is much to learn from observing growing fruits. When you sip in their health values, let yourself be reminded of something special about the essence of the vines, tree branches and flowering bushes that offer them to you.

Fruit Categories and Their Health Benefits

Sub-Acid Fruits

Apples. Moist, crunchy apples contain soluble fiber (pectin) which is effective in lowering cholesterol. They tend to stimulate the body's digestive secretions and are beneficial for a sluggish liver, constipation and conditions of overweight.

Pears. Mellow, sweet, juicy pears are recommended for stimulating digestion and soothing an inflamed colon (colitis). They help to alkalinize the blood as well.

Apricots. This delightful orange fruit is high in iron and minerals as well as vitamin A. Apricots will cleanse impurities from the blood and help overcome anemia. They are also said to help ease inflammation of the bronchial tubes.

Peaches. The vitamins and minerals in peaches make this juicy fruit valuable for anemia, sluggish digestion and over-acid conditions in the blood. They have long been said to improve the health and color of the skin and complexion.

Plums. Plums are great energizers of the intestinal tract, having mild laxative properties and the ability to relieve gas and even hemmorhoids. By cleansing the intestines, plums benefit the whole body.

Cherries. Iron- and magnesium-rich cherries are a great cleanser of the kidneys, urinary system and the liver. They are reported to be valuable in cases of anemia, under-nourished blood, high blood pressure and rheumatism.

Grapes. Whether purple or green, grapes provide natural sugars to the body. In addition to being a quick energizer, they are a potent cleanser of the entire body, especially the kidneys and liver.

Hint—To ripen peaches, nectarines and pears, place them in a brown paper bag. Close bag loosely and leave at room temperature. This speeds up and improves natural ripening. Check for ripeness by placing fruit in your palm and squeezing gently. It should "give" to light pressure. When fragrant, it is ready to eat or to be placed in your refrigerator.

Acid Fruits

Strawberries. Plump, red and juicy strawberries are cleansing in nature, helping to rid the bloodstream, intestines and liver of toxins. Strawberries are also said to benefit stiff joints and ease cattarh in the system.

Raspberries. This delicate, rose-colored fruit is a delicious source of vitamins A and C. Remember raspberries for their ability to help correct constipation, obesity and high blood pressure.

Cranberries. This bright-scarlet berry is helpful to the kidneys and bladder because its natural acidity creates an environment in which bacteria cannot easily thrive. Also, consider this as a fruit to clarify the complexion.

Blueberries. Blueberries are known as a blood cleanser. They are a natural choice if one needs to correct either diarrhea or constipation. (Their antiseptic value helps ease inflammation.) Anemia and menstrual disorders are also said to benefit from this fruit.

Kiwi. A fuzzy, brown-skinned fruit with bright green flesh, kiwi is sweet yet slightly tart. Ounce-for-ounce, it is higher in vitamin C than most other fruits.

Lemon. As a natural antiseptic, the juice of lemon is a powerful cleanser of the entire system.

Oranges. Oranges have been recommended to alleviate many ailments including lung problems, high blood pressure, obesity and vitamin C deficiency.

Hints—Acid and sub-acid fruits can be combined with nuts and seeds for flavor, texture and digestive compatibility. However, you might consider some combos an exception.

Exotic Fruits

Papaya. Containing the enzyme papain, this fruit is valuable for tuning up the digestive system. The juice and fruit of papaya seek out cellular waste and mucous in the stomach and colon.

Mango. Like papaya, mangoes are said to strengthen poor digestion and overcome acidity in the body. Mangoes also are beneficial for inflamed kidneys. They contain a rich supply of beta carotene.

Cactus Pear. Also known as Indian pear or prickly pear, this pinkish-green, spiny-skinned fruit is rich in natural sugars and of a refreshing fuchsia color.

Cantaloupe. Also known as muskmelon, this low-calorie fruit is rich in vitamins (C and A) and minerals, including potassium. Cantaloupe is recommended for correcting obesity, sluggish bowel, blood deficiencies and stiff joints.

Avocado. This soft-green fruit is gentle on the intestines and stomach. Providing healthful fatty acids, vitamins and minerals (such as potassium), it is a great food for bulding the body and nourishing the appearance of the skin.

*Hint—Melons are most friendly to the digestive tract when eaten alone, or in the morning before many foods have been introduced to the digestive tract. They digest very quickly and do not favor being held up with other foods in the stomach. Fruit juice and melon make a nice combination. Sometimes a hint of another fruit can serve as a spice rather than as a competing ingredient.

Sweet fruits and dried fruits

Bananas. When ripe (usually visible by the presence of brown freckles on their skin), bananas are a potassium-rich fruit that gives quick, yet sustained energy. Consider them valuable for healing ulcers, colitis and diarrhea. Red bananas turn slightly purplish as they ripen to a sweet flavor. To freeze bananas for recipes, simply peel ripe fruit and place in freezer bags.

Plantain. Resembling large, fat, green bananas, plantains are relatives of bananas and have a high starch content. They are a healthful source of vitamin C and beta carotene. Plantain and red banana can be sautéed in a bit of water and ghee for a dessert-like Smoothie.

Dates. Dates are among the very sweetest of fruits, providing an energy-giving source of carbohydrates, dietary fiber, iron and potassium.

Raisins and Currants. Dried grapes are concentrated bites of vitamins, minerals (iron and potassium) and fiber (soluble and insoluble). Raisins have as much iron by weight as cooked legumes or red meat. Both raisins and currants are valuable strength-building foods that can also help correct anemia, low blood pressure and constipation.

Figs. Noted for their delightful sweetness and soft texture, figs are rich in dietary fiber (9 grams in 3.5 ounces) as well as calcium. They are said to provide (17 percent) more calcium than skim milk. Figs are also a great source of potassium and iron. The drinks herein feature Calymirna figs, a Turkish variety that is commonly imported in its dried state. Keep figs tightly wrapped or stored in air-tight jars in the refrigerator.

Prunes. Bred from an extra-sweet, fleshy variety of plums, prunes are a rich, yet mellow-tasting fruit that is exceptionally high in fiber—the custodian of the digestive tract. Ounce for ounce, prunes contain more soluble fiber than dried beans, fruits and vegetables! They are also rich in energy-giving iron, vitamins, potassium and beta carotene.

*Hint—Sweet and dried fruits complement Smoothies that feature starchy grains. However, I don't combine acid fruits with grains, because their acids cancel out the digestive enzymes required for starch breakdown.

Dried Fruits

In addition to using fresh fruits in recipes, you will not want to overlook the delicious option of rehydrating dried fruit.

Drying a fruit reduces its water content, and its minerals and natural sugars seem to multiply. When reconstituted, however, you have a juicy food that offers creamy texture to recipes, as well as delightful flavor and energy values.

Some of the dried fruits I favor using include: pears, dates, currants, apples, raisins and apricots. Many food cooperatives stock varieties that are free of sulfite, an undesirable preservative that may cause allergic reactions in some people.

Dried fruits store well in refrigerator jars or plastic bags. However, they have a tendency at times to become moldy.

To rehydrate fruit overnight:

Fill a pint-sized jar with about one cup of dried fruit. Fill the jar with water or juice. If you have soaked more fruit than is needed in your recipe, use the remaining portion within one week's time.

To instantly rehydrate fruit:

Place fruit (amount specified in recipe) in a small mixing bowl or dish. Cover fruit with near-boiling water, then increase the amount an inch or two more. Wait three to fifteen minutes for fruits to soften.

Nuts and Seeds

I use nuts and seeds sparingly in Smoothie recipes, because even in small amounts, they have so much to offer in the way of distinctive flavors, textures and nutrients.

It's hard to imagine that nuts have flourished from the plains to the tropics for as many as 60 million years. Yet it is inspiring to know that civilizations once depended on them for staple nourishment for which they took the place of grains and other foods.

The nuts featured in my recipes aren't actually what botanists consider true nuts (*i.e.*, single seeded "fruits" such as acorns and beechnuts, which possess inedible skins). Rather, they are the sweet and fleshy relatives of nut trees which yield almonds, pecans, walnuts, cashews and pine nuts. I love to jumble them all together and curiously sample their convoluted shapes, flavors and textures as well as their pretty earthen colors—tawny, brown, cream and golden.

Although most people shy away from nuts because of a belief that they are fattening, there is now substantial scientific evidence that our bodies need the kind of essential fatty acids (linoleic, linolenic and arachidonic acids) found in nuts. This trio aids the body in burning fat and lowering cholesterol.

Nuts are also shown to be rich in lipo-busting

amino acids such as tyrosine, phenalaynine and arginine.

Besides possesing healthful fats, nuts contain protein and minerals. Calcium, magnesium, phosphorus, zinc, copper, selenium, potassium and iron provide nourishment for the teeth and gums as well as the muscles of the entire body.

Similarly, seeds which flourish on such flowering plants as sunflower, squash and sesame provide these same minerals in addition to fluorine and iodine. A large percentage of their calories come from protein. For example, an ounce of sesame seeds is said to contain as many calories as three ounces of meat.

Whether you choose to buy nuts in the shell or unshelled, is mostly a matter of convenience.

Nuts keep better within their shell, but of course they then require cracking, which takes more time and finesse than many of us seem to have. The fact that nuts are so difficult to crack hints at a secret about their preciousness. Mother Nature has packaged them carefully so as to suggest that we realize their perishability.

Have you ever seen an almond orchard up close? The bearers of the crunchy fruit are about twenty feet tall, blossoming with pink and white flowers that appear before their leaves do. The unshelled nuts rest inside a gracefully fitted vest which manages to resemble a flattened, greenish peach. When the entire fruit ripens, it dries and splits its vest open further, revealing the nut in its second skin.

Once the textured shell covering the edible fruit is removed, it begins to absorb the oxygen which encourages its rancidity.

To prevent nuts from aging prematurely, I always keep them refrigerated in airtight glass jars. Nature will make her freshest and most favorable impression on your tastebuds when you sample the organically raised nuts and seeds (as well as nut butters) that are now commonly available. (See the directory in this book.)

Take pleasure in the benefits that fresh raw nuts and seeds can lend to your body!

Vegetables

Do Smoothies that are enriched with vegetables taste as sumptuous and rich as fruity ones do? Yes! And I'm delighted to suggest some of the veggies that yield so well to a blender's cutting blades and which create the kind of nourishment that adapts to being a breakfast, snack or dessert.

If you're striving to squeeze three to five servings (the recommended quota) of garden-grown produce into your daily menu, the taste of vegetables seasoned with herbs or sweetened with spices can inspire even vegetable haters to reach this goal.

Vegetables are a "must" for balanced health and well-being. Besides being artful renditions that feed the senses, they supply nearly all of the vitamins and minerals needed by the body.

And one can't rave enough about their fiber content, a true custodian of the digestive tract.

Some vegetables, such as carrots and squash, can enrich Smoothies with carbohydrates, which are the body's principal source of energy.

Combining them with protein from other plant foods is a way to pack in energy-giving values in food combinations that are easy to digest.

Many of the vegetables my recipes feature are technically considered fruits, because the fleshy part of them contains seeds. Tomatoes, squashes and peppers are a few examples.

The botanical families used to classify different

types of vegetables include: leaves, roots, pods, stalks, and fruit vegetables.

To develop an intuitive sense of the kind of energy that vegetables possess, find a comfortable spot in your garden to sit, look around and listen.

If a garden isn't accessible, simply harvest an assortment of vegetables from your local food co-op or store and spread them atop your kitchen table.

Notice the look of dewy lightness and fluid movement in leafy foods such as Romaine, spinach, bok choy, watercress, etc. These are the foods that burst through the soil and reached skyward to the sun. Their leaves sometimes appear as fins or fans, breathing in the oxygen around them.

Next, enjoy the contrast of a densely woven *root* vegetable such as carrot, beet or sweet potato. Dusted with black dirt as they are scooped from a season of hibernation in the earth, do they not seem to convey a sturdy, solid, "building block" kind of nourishment?

Caress the shiny luminous skin of a plump tomato, or the decorative dermis of squashes, pumpkin or zuchinni. Open up their fleshy moist contents. They are pregnant with the seeds of reproduction, and you may wonder, as I do, if they aren't a feminine version of vegetable life.

Quite uniquely, our vegetable foods grow above ground and below, as well as in between. Could it be that their positions of growth are offering to help us fathom how they can nourish different parts of ourselves?

Each day, more and more healing values are being discovered in our foods and proven by science to affect the health of our organs. What we are being taught, we might also learn to validate through our senses as well.

Enjoy the many healing benefits found in the following vegetables that make unique contributions to Smoothie recipes.

Artichokes (Bud)

Commercially packaged (plain or marinated) artichoke hearts in a jar are occasionally used in recipes. They offer a quick and easy way to experience the meaty delicacy of this intricately structured food, which is rich in vitamin C and fiber.

Beets (Root)

Although noted for their sweetness, beets are low in calories. Beet juice may be used sparingly in a recipe as a color or flavor accent (try with pineapple or apple). It is rich in minerals such as iron, and even small amounts will do a remarkable job of cleansing the liver, building the blood, serving as a diuretic and menstrual regulator.

Carrots (Root)

Carrot juice (versus the whole fibrous vegetable) is accented in Smoothies. It contains practically every mineral your body could ask for, including calcium, iron and magnesium, which are blood builders. It is a reliable blood cleanser, cholesterol reducer and spleen-pancreas builder. This coupled organ is nourished by the sweet flavor occuring naturally in whole foods. The liver also benefits tremendously from carrot juice, which in turn strengthens digestion. Beta carotene, a cancer preventative, is in rich supply in carrots as well.

Celery (Stalk)

Organic sodium, the element in fresh ribs of celery, acts as a solvent in the body. It can be experienced by the kidneys and joints as it helps to break down calcium deposits that so often lodge there. Celery is also rich in magnesium (a relaxant) and iron. It blends well with a cocktail of other veggie juices.

Cucumber (Leafy vine)

Feed your hair and nails with organically raised cucumbers. They are rich in silicon and flourine, as well as other minerals which add refreshing low calories, flavor and fiber to summertime vegetable cocktails or Smoothies.

Corn (Stalk)

A high carbohydrate food that is nourishing to the heart, I use summer's fresh, sweet corn kernels, (from leftover meals) to flavor a Smoothie. Canned corn (vacuum-packed in water) can also be used and is equal in nutrient value to fresh. The corn plant is actually a grass and the kernels themselves a grain. But most people think of sweet corn (versus field corn raised for animals) as a vegetable.

Peppers

Whether they have bell-shaped lobes of green, yellow, orange or red, peppers are loaded with vitamin C (green varieties have as much as two times more than citrus fruit). Their minerals (flourine and silicon) nourish hair, skin and nails. Peppers have been known to combat obesity, constipation, high blood pressure and acid conditions in the body. Ranging from slightly sweet in flavor (red) to pungent and hot, you'll want to choose carefully before adding their juice or fiber to Smoothies.

Pumpkin (Ground Vine)

Since the big orange pumpkins used on Halloween are often too stringy to eat, "sugar pumpkins," a smaller, sweeter variety with smooth flesh are better. I prefer the ease of using canned pumpkin (such as Festal brand). Fresh pumpkin is only available in the fall and winter. This orange fruit-vegetable is rich in energy-giving carbos, fiber and vitamin A. Pumpkin is said to be good for eliminating excess fluids in the body's tissues and is soothing to inflamed intestinal and stomach conditions.

Spinach (Leafy)

The deep-green leaves of the plant are a true friend to the digestive tract when eaten raw, as they stimulate the peristaltic action of the intestine. Spinach is also high in iron, beta carotene, minerals and plant protein, which can ease conditions of anemia and fatigue.

Sweet Potato (Yams)

These tuberous roots are among the most nutritious and easy-to-digest foods in the vegetable kingdom. A medium-size potato contains about 120 calories and 20,000 I.U. of vitamin A. Consider this food beneficial for healing conditions such as stomach ulcers, inflamed colon, diarrhea, low blood pressure and wasting diseases. Sweet potatoes have a natural sweetness produced by an enzyme in the potato that converts the starches into sugars as it matures. Oranged-fleshed varieties as well as yellow ones, are available at most food co-ops and farmer's markets. I prefer organically raised ones with smooth, unbruised, unsprayed skins (fungicides are often used and can affect the flavor, etc.). The orange (moist) variety is somewhat sweeter than the yellow (dry) type. Sweet potatos are also called yams, yet true yams are seldom available in this country. The term yam is often accepted when referring to the sweet potato.

To prepare:

Wash and prick potatos with a knife. Bake in a (400-degree oven for 30-45 minutes, depending on their size). Or, place two to four potatoes in a microwave oven for about 10-15 minutes. Cool at room temperature, then place in refrigerator to chill if recipe requires. Potatoes keep well for two to three days in the refrigerator.

Tomato

Although botanically a fruit (technically considered a berry), the tomato is served as a vegetable. All types of tomatoes are excellent source of vitamin C and beta carotene.

Winter Squash (Ground Vine)

Buttercup, butternut, delicata, golden nugget, Hubbard, golden acorn, and turban are some of the many varities of squash recognized by their tough, protective shells and their ability to keep well. The yellow or orange flesh of squashes is more nutritious than the watery flesh of summer sqaush, such as zuchinni. A 3.5 ounce serving of Hubbard or butternut squash will supply 100 percent of the RDA of vitamin A. For Smoothie recipes, experiment with whatever squash you happen to have on hand. I prefer to bake (vs. boil) squash because this cooking method preserves the sweetness and conserves its vitamin content.

To bake:

Halve squash lengthwise and scoop out seeds and strings. Place squash, cut-side down in a foil-lined baking pan. Pour one-fourth inch of water in pan. Cover with foil and bake at 350-400 degrees (about 40 minutes) until tender when pierced with a knife. Smaller squashes may require shorter cooking times.

Grains

Since whole grains are among the best sources of complex carbohydrates and have a nutritional figure that is endowed with bran, germ and endosperm, they add fantastic enrichment to Smoothies.

If you've ever hoped to get such nourishment from refined "carbos" such as bread, instant cereal, bagels, chips and crackers, etc., you may have discovered they don't build bodies as well as a steaming bowl of oats or a side of pilaf.

When you make whole grains a part of your daily diet, it becomes easy to imagine how the sturdy, cooked morsels can add "body" to a blender drink, as well as to your physique.

As you probably know, bran—the outer coat of a grain—contains most of its soluble and insoluble fiber. The soluble part of grain has gained a good reputation for lowering cholesterol. The insoluble portion helps regulate the rate at

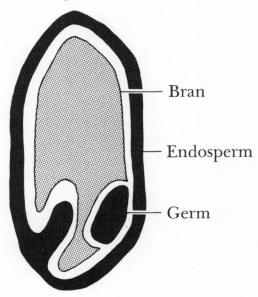

Bran

Endosperm

Germ

which food is digested, monitoring blood sugar in the process as well as discouraging constipation.

Housed within the germ of a grain are significant amounts of vitamins E and B, which help to maintain the function of the heart and circulatory system, as well the nervous system.

Carbohydrates, proteins and minerals constitute the grain's endosperm, which delivers flavor and texture to our tastebuds.

The grains that are featured in my recipes, include both true grains and pseudo-grains. Barley, rice, teff, and corn are a few the true cereal grasses, which, in my expierience, blend favorably with other ingredients without giving the overt impression of being starchy.

Quinoa and amaranth are pseudo-grains, yet their makeup is similar enough to a true grain to offer its entire benefits.

The term "grain" has long referred to many kinds of cereal grasses, and especially to their small, seedlike "fruit"—the kernel. The kernel is technically indeed a complete "fruit" that sometimes bears a husk. Cereal grains are considered to be the most highly developed of all the seeds of food plants because they have the capacity to reproduce in such extravagant abundance.

Whether grains flourish in a field, a paddy or atop a mountain, they are a beautiful sight to behold. Like a graceful sea, each mature seedling seems to flow in unity with the rest. It is apparent that some grains are linked to the sun (millet, corn and quinoa) while a grain like rice, which grows in watery soil is akin to the moon and the earth.

I like to believe that these qualities in a grain have

a part in nourishing the feminine and masculine balance within us.

All in all, grains can bring greater continuity and strength to our lives as they connect us to our global heritage. The Incas, the Ethiopians, as well as the early civilizations that were once the caretakers of these ancient plants, have "reappeared," as it were, to nourish modern man's changing nutritional needs.

By choosing to eat more grains, we satisfy the body's needs for protein without having to rely on animal sources.

Round out your diet with Smoothies featuring whole grains and experience their special health values.

Amaranth

Often considered Indian food (where it is grown today in Mexico and South-Central America), amaranth is an eight-thousand-year-old food staple of the ancient Aztec culture. It comes from a very tall, broad-leafed plant (not a grain) bearing brightly colored flowers. The itty bitty seeds (a pound may contain 500,000 or more) can be cooked like breakfast cereal. It has a strong, earthy and sweet, corn-like essence. Amaranth's distinctive flavor lends itself to accents of sweet maple, banana, raisin, etc.. It is high in protein, calcium, iron and vitamins A and C. Low in gluten, it can be appreciated by allergy sufferers.

Barley

From Scotland to Ethiopia, barley has long been grown around the world. Like oats, barley is an excellent source of soluble fiber effective in lowering cholesterol. It is also effective in increasing body weight in a healthy way, and is mild enough to help heal stomach ulcers and diarrhea. Hulled barley has its bran intact and contains many minerals, including iron and thiamine. Pearled barley, the ivory-colored version, has its husk and bran removed but retains a delicate and pleasantly nourishing appeal; it cooks quickly and purees easily.

Rice (Short-Grain)

Short-grain rice is oval in shape and has the highest percentage of the starch that makes rice stick and clump together when cooked. Although rice is grown on almost every continent (except Antarctica), China produces 90 percent of the world's crop. Rice thrives in warm climates with an abundance of fresh water.

The type of rice grown in the United States is paddy rice, which is cultivated from fields that have been flooded during the growing season. Upland rice can be grown in wet soil.

Rice is a great source of B vitamins, iron, phosphorus, magnesium and is balancing food. Rice milk is used in many recipes, but you may want to experiment with short-grain rice as a fortifier and texturizer.

Quinoa (pronounced Keen-wa)

This hardy food was once the staple food of the ancient Incas. It has one of the finest sources of protein in the entire plant kingdom, with a ratio of amino acids that constitutes a complete protein. When cooked, it has a light nut-like flavor, and it purees smoothly in recipes. Consider quinoa a real body builder!

Teff

The tiniest grain in the world, teff has offered sustenance to many people, such as the Ethiopians. It cooks up like a sweet, molasses-flavored malto-meal. Ounce for ounce, it has more nutrient-rich bran and germ than any other grain. Having a smooth yet grainy appeal, it is best used in small amounts as a texturizing accent.

Tapioca

Tapioca is not a grain, but I have included it here because it is cooked in liquid (as are grains) and is considered a carbohydrate, or starch. Juice pressed from the root of the herbal plant, cassava, becomes tapioca pearls when it is heated on plates or dried in the sun. Tapioca is valued as a light and nutritious food for convalescing persons whose stomach or intestines may not be well. Cooked in water or diluted fruit juice (such as apple or pear), tapioca is low-cal and lucious. It is digested easily enough to complement juicy fruits such as berries and peaches.

To make dairy free tapioca—

Combine:

2¼ cups apple juice
¼ cup quick-cooking tapioca pearls
2 Tbls. honey

Combine the the juice and tapioca in a sauce pan. Let stand 5 to 10 minutes. Bring to boil over medium heat, stirring often. When mixture reaches a boil, remove from heat and allow to cool for about 20 minutes. Stir well and flavor with vanilla if desired. Chill in refigerator.

Hints—Cooking times and procedures for grains vary. Follow instructions found on packaged varieties of the aforementioned grains. Grains combine best with recipes that feature sweet or dried (hydrated) fruits, versus acid fruits, which do not harmonize with grains from a digestive standpoint.

Wholesome Sweeteners

There are many special places where Mother Nature wears her subtle yet all-encompassing perfume. To catch a whiff of it, simply unscrew the caps from jars of golden and amber-colored honey, rice and maple syrups wherefrom her blossoms, fields, and trees exude the fragrance.

Then dip your finger in, and dab the nectar onto your tastebuds. A little sweetness always melts divinely, doesn't it?

Yet it appears that all the world's fantasies about this flavor can never be realized as long as there are artificial contenders to entice our better judgment. A friend of mine recently confided that she preferred to punctuate her diet with the likes of Nutra-Sweet and Equal. In her mind, these items were a svelte substitute for sugar and its unhealthy side effects. She had a point.

But not being one to rave over a test-tube substance's ability "to turn food marvel," I wondered out loud about the kind of chemistry such non-nutritive elements would induce in her body. Something like a high, shrill-pitched noise replaced any rational explanation.

All I could think of was the contrast of the thin-flowing sweeteners I cherished, made from energy-giving whole foods. I shared with my friend, the fact that whole grains of rice were used to prepare mellow-sweet rice syrup. And that mineral-rich pods of carob were added to iron-rich molasses to create carob molasses syrup.

I told her about an herbaceous shrub named Stevia that had only one calorie per ten leaves. Lastly, I must have communicated how these "foods" lend me the chance to experience every bit of nature's splendor.

This earthy perspective was well recieved as my friend considered measuring her desire for better food choices in terms of their whole-food benefits versus only calories.

I was delighted to recently get a call from this person, relating her enthusiasm and contentment at having tried several of these new sweeteners in recipes.

Each of the liquid and granular sweetners introduced below invite you to do the same. I feel confident about saying that they can nourish your cravings—not make small "monsters" out of them as many refined and artificial sweetners have been known to do.

Liquid Sweeteners

Rice Syrup

This is a delectable liquid sweetener, pale-blonde in color, resembling honey in texture and visual appeal. Rice syrup is made from organic brown rice. It is first ground into a meal, then cooked before natural cereal enzymes are added which convert the starches in the rice to complex natural sugars. A sweet liquid is squeezed from the mixture and cooked briefly until it thickens. This is truly a healthful sweetener since the body does not need to release extra insulin in order to break down the malted grain. Rice syrup is the perfect complement to recipes featuring grains and starchy fruits, as well as "fruit-vegetables" such as squash. I also use it in sweet potato combos and fresh fruit-and-nut blends.

Barley Malt Syrup

Barley malt syrup is a dark amber-colored syrup resembling a duo of flavors—perhaps rice syrup and molasses combined. It is made from barley grains in the same tradition as rice syrup and is delicious in Smoothies featuring grains, bananas and pumpkin.

Honey

Because of its taste, texture and overall availability, honey is a reliable sweetening ingredient for just about any recipe herein. Honey varies in texture, flavor and color, depending on the kinds of flowers from which the nectar is gathered. As a rule, dark honeys are more nutritionally potent than light honeys, although they impart a stronger flavor.

Since honey is almost twice as sweet as cane sugar, smaller amounts of it are needed for sweetening purposes. Unfiltered, raw honey contains carbohydrates in the form of sugars, small amounts of minerals, B vitamins, as well as vitamins C, D, and E.

Honey can be used alone in recipes, or combined with other sweeteners such as carob, molasses or maple syrup. You can also substitute half or more of the amount of honey in a recipe with a dry powdered sweetener such as barley malt powder. A dash of it replaces two teaspoons of sugar.

Maple Syrup

Good quality maple syrup (such as some authentic Canadian and Vermont versions, as well as syrup from small producers) can serve as a delicious addition to Smoothies. Although it is not particularly abundant in specific nutritional values, it does contain natural sugars, which, when used in moderation, can furnish quick energy to the body.

Be advised that most of the commercial varieties of maple syrup contain salt, chemical preservatives, defoaming agents, or formaldehyde (from the pellets used to tap the trees).

Pure Carob Molasses Syrup

This dark, flowing brown syrup, is made by combining molasses with carob powder. If you've never been particularly keen about eating molasses on its own, you'll love it in this simple Lebanese recipe. It tastes mellow, yet distinctly sweet. Kids often think it has the appeal of chocolate. You'll want to experiment with this iron and mineral-rich product in recipes that feature such fruits as bananas and raisins, combined with barley, sesame or quinoa. Check your neighborhood Lebanese grocery mart for this product.

Powdered Sweeteners

Barley Malt Powder

Barley malt powder is derived from grains that have been sprouted, dried and cooked down to a natural malt. "Dr. Bronners" (brand name) powder contains a uniquely sweet blend of barley malt, orange juice solids, calcium magnesium phosphate, parsley, chia seeds, vegetable protein, dulse, sea lettuce, lemon juice solids, potassium salt, rosehips, anise and mint.

One part barley malt replaces twenty parts sugar. A dash has only three calories and substitutes for two teaspoons of sugar, giving you a reduction of up to 98 percent of the usual calories, without sacrificing sweetness. Barley malt powder, can be used in place of, or in conjunction with liquid sweeteners. This way you can reduce the amount of liquid sweeteners and stretch the flavor you desire.

Stevia Rebaudiana (Sweet Leaf) Powder

Stevia is an herbal sweetener, derived from a small shrub grown in Brazil and Argentina, and now in the southwestern part of the United States. If you are on a restricted-sugar meal plan, this is an ingredient you'll want to look into. Stevia's sweetening power is thirty to eighty times that of sugar, yet it has only one calorie per ten leaves. It can be used in the same way barley malt powder is used. A pinch per cup of liquid will do. Sweet leaf has a licorice-like taste that may not complement every kind of recipe.

Yet it may be worth your while to experiment with it when you consider its unique health properties. South American Indians have used this sweetener for centuries. It is said to have regulating effects on the blood sugar, as well an inhibitory influence on bacteria in the mouth and a tonifying effect which positively affects the metabolism. It also contains anti-yeast, anti-bacterial and anti-fungus properties.

Sucanat (Trade Name)

Resembling brown sugar in taste and appeal, Sucanat is the trade name given to a 100 percent organic granulated sugar-cane juice. Unrefined, it is considered to be a healthy alternative to refined sugar. Sucanat supplies sweet-tasting, easy-to-utilize minerals and vitamins (namely calcium, phosphorus, potassium, chromium, magnesium, iron and vitamins A and C). It tastes "just right" in Smoothies featuring grains, pumpkins, squashes, bananas, and dried fruits which have been rehydrated.

Flavoring Essences, Spices and Herbs

Flavoring Essences

Flavoring essences gathered from natural herbs, spices, veggies and fruits add much to the appeal of Smoothie recipes. I like to rely on the natural, non-imitation varieties of both flavorings and extracts that are available in most natural food grocery stores.

Frontier brand has an extensive alcohol-free selection of flavors ranging from orange, banana, cherry and pineapple, to almond, vanilla, cinnamon, coconut and butterscotch. Choice brand, is another variety of flavoring extracts. These delightful flavors come in handy when you want to achieve a flavor but don't have the food ingredient on hand. Essences also bring out the sweetness in drinks and make it more definitive. The amount of flavoring extracts in a recipe may vary depending on the strength of the brand used.

Spices and Herbs

Some of the spices I use in recipes include cinnamon, coriander, allspice, nutmeg, anise and cardamom. Spices have a long and unique history in

many cultures of the world. To catch my nostrils meeting the edge of a spice jar containing cardamom on several occasions while writing this book, I realize it was propped in front of me for its aromatherapeutic value. It invigorated my thinking process in much the same way that incense might clarify a room. Spices do indeed have medicinal values that shouldn't be overlooked.

To give you an idea, cinnamon is recommended by many herbalists for aiding digestion. Studies by Japanese researchers show that cinnamon also contains a substance that acts on certain fungi, parasites, and bacteria, including botulinus. Anise and coriander seeds are also spices that offer to soothe an upset stomach, aid digestion and relieve gas.

Culinary herbs have medicinal qualities as well. Mint, dill, chives, cilantro and parsley are some of the easy-to-grow herbs with which I spike vegetable Smoothies.

Dill has a way of quickly relieving wind in the intestines, and mint will do the same while it also encourages relief from indigestion and bad breath.

Parsley and chives are well known for their stimulating affect on the kidneys as well as the digestive juices. In short, drinking and nibbling on herbs and spices is an appetizing way to assist the body's functions.

Nature's 'Super Foods'

Smoothie Fortifiers

Beyond fruits, veggies, nuts, seeds, grains, sweeteners and spices, what more could you possibly want to add to a Smoothie recipe?

"Ask your body" to tell you! If it's lean muscle with which you are striving to replace fat, why not add a tablespoon of flaxseed meal? Simply enjoy its nutty flavor and fabulous fiber while it goes to work in your body, lowering cholesterol and dispersing the bad fats. If you feel more lively after a routine with this ingredient, you might chalk it up to the fact that flaxseed is also instrumental in boosting the immune system and regulating the body's hormonal output.

Speaking of hormones (the stuff of youthfulness), maybe your body would care for some enzymes, which offer to stave off fatigue and premature aging. I've experienced almost instant benefits from such fortifiers as royal jelly and pollen, products that bees gather for their own food and fertility.

How about when you're craving some light protein, with concentrated food values? Golden-yellow nutritional yeast powder or deep-green barley grass extract can be easily stirred into your beverage—for dynamic nutrients. I refer to many of my favorite fortifiers as *whole weight* body-building elements. Because they originate from nature in their whole, singular state and undergo little or no processing, they offer to be digested naturally and easily.

When any foodstuff is digested efficiently, it can better nourish the whole body—including organs, tissues, cells and bloodstream (versus only the muscles). Yet when it isn't, the byproducts of its indigestion get stored away. Then, toxic pockets can form the congestive residues that lead to overweight.

Food fortifiers such as the ones listed below, are a light source of enrichment aimed at nourishing your whole self.

Granular Fortifiers

Bee Pollen

Pollen granules are tiny, potent, golden food nuggets that are gathered from all kinds of flowering plants by worker bees. The flowers' fertilizing element, pollen, gives as the benefit of a sun-potent food rich in natural sugars, vitamins, minerals, trace elements, amino acids and an estimated 5,000 enzymes. Pollen tastes rather potent as well. If adding it directly to a recipe doesn't appeal to you, simply sprinkle it on top of the drink or chase it down with your Smoothie.

Chia Seeds

These tiny, charcoal-colored seeds were eaten in many Indian civilizations whenever people went on long hunts or migrations. They are actually a relative of the mint (herb) family. You might care to add one ground teaspoon per cup of liquid. The seeds become mucilaginous when blended with liquid. Try with raisins, figs, currants and berries.

Lecithin Granules

Lecithin, is a soft, yellow food supplement extracted from the soybean. It is a superb emulsifier of fats. A natural constituent of every cell in the human body, lecithin is found in the myelin sheath, or fatty protective covering for the nerves. Lecithin will help dissolve cholesterol deposits on the arterial walls, aiding in the prevention of heart disease. Use a pinch of lecithin in recipes that feature nuts. It will enhance their digestibility.

Flaxseeds

Derived from a lovely blue flowering plant that graces summer fields along paths all the way from the northern United States and Canada to Europe, flaxseed is a multipurpose herb.

Flaxseeds are available in two colors, glossy golden and shiny chocolate brown. When the seed is ground, it blends easily with other ingredients, especially bananas, raisins and dates. It releases a healing mucilage when combined with wet ingredients and is quite capable of replacing laxative products such as Metamucel.

Flaxseed also contains essential fatty acids (namely omega 3 and 6) that the body can't make on its own. These fatty acids reduce serum tryglycerides (or hard transfats as they are sometimes called), reducing or eliminating the likelihood of atherosclerosis and high cholesterol. Flax is also shown to have a positive effect on the immune system. I love its calcium content, and the way it seems to nourish skin from the inside out.

Gomasio

Gomasio powder is a simple natural food condiment made from toasted sesame seeds and unrefined sea salt. It has a deliciously light and nutty flavor that's rich in protein & calcium. Try it sprinkled atop a vegetable Smoothie.

Liquid Fortifiers

Flaxseed Oil

Flaxseed oil, from the seed itself, is one of the best of oils in the diet. It is the richest and purest source of alpha linolenic acid. Spoon it from the bottle as is (refrigerated). Its fresh-pressed flavor, aroma and appearance, which includes a translucent, golden orange hue, is due to its natural beta carotene.

Royal Jelly

Royal jelly is a substance produced by worker bees. When fed to an ordinary female bee in the larval stage, miraculous transformations occur. She will become the queen bee and grow to one and one-half times her normal size. She becomes fertile, lays over twice her weight in eggs in a single day, and lives over five years (other bees live only a few weeks). Her exclusive diet of royal jelly is what creates the difference between her and the thousands of other bees in the hive.

You'll want to check your health food store for royal jelly (often combined with honey), which looks like a pearlescent-colored honey.

It is one of the richest sources of pantothenic acid (vitamin B_5) as well as all the eight essential amino acids—especially tyrosine and tryptophan. It is known to be very therapeutic during periods of convalescence or at any time extra strength and nourishment are needed. Relish a spoonful or dropper full at the same time you drink your Smoothies, or try mixing its essence in fruity drinks, such as those fortified with tapioca.

Soy Amino Bouillon

A few amino bouillons are available on the market. Bragg's and Dr. Bronner's are two brand names that I enjoy. Ingredients such as soybeans, molasses, vitamin C, lemon and orange juice solids, ocean dulse, soy lecithin, dulse and papain enzyme characterize these bouillons, which are rich in amino acids, the building blocks of protein. Try them in vegetable-juice Smoothies, like carrot juice or tomato mixed with avocado.

Tamari Bouillon

Tamari is the original Japanese soy sauce. It is made entirely from soybeans whose content of amino acids causes the development of its deep, rich flavor during the fermentation process. Try it in vegetable Smoothies.

Miso

Miso is a creamy food paste made from cultured rice, soybeans, water and sea salt. Its full-bodied taste is a curious blend of sweet and salty. Because it is fermented, it is rich in vitamin B_{12}, which helps combat anemia. Miso also absorbs and deactivates toxins in the intestinal tract. You might care to experiment with it in tomato juice type beverages.

Powdered Fortifiers

Carob Powder

Carob powder is a sweet and delicious chocolate-like powder from the fruit (pod) of an evergreen tree indigenous to the Mediterranean region. It is a satisfying substitute for cocoa powder, although it can be combined with cocoa for extra, authentic chocolate flavor. Carob contains a fair share of protein, natural sugar, calcium, minerals and B vitamins. Carob mixes well in Smoothies containing bananas and grains.

Cafix Roasted Cereal Beverage Powder

Cafix is the name given to a product that resembles instant coffee. Its caffeine-free, non-addictive ingredients include mineral-rich (iron) roasted barley, rye, chicory, and shredded beet roots. Try it in recipes featuring food flavors of mint, soy, carob and grains.

Slippery Elm Powder

Elm powder is derived from the inner bark of the deciduous elm tree, cultivated in North America. It has a light and fluffy texture, is pale beige in color, and may remind you of a protein powder with a maple-like aromatic quality. Slippery elm has many enzymes that aid in the body's digestive process. Its mucilage is soothing to coughs, stomach and bowel troubles, as well as the urinary tract. Taste it in frosty Smoothies featuring nondairy ices and sweet fruits. (See "Frosty Apple Cinamon Swirl" and "Banana Maple Pecan.")

Nutritional Yeast Flakes

Nutritional yeast powder, an edible yeast grown on blackstrap molasses, is a flavorful yellow powder with a nutty cheesy taste. It supplies a bundle of B vitamins and minerals and is often considered a beauty and nerve food. A teaspoon or two per cup of liquid won't overpower Smoothies containing acid fruits (berries, apples or tomatoes).

Dulse Flakes/Powder

Sea vegetable powders are made in the Japanese tradition, from dried seaweed harvested in seaport markets. Flavors such as sea salt and garlic are added to some brands which enhance their slightly nutty, bean-like flavor. Sprinkle in (or on top of) vegetable cocktail Smoothies.

Beet Juice Powder

Beet juice powder is made from the freshly extracted juice of organically grown beets dried with arrowroot. Its bright fuchsia color and earthy flavor seem to agree nicely with the flavors of apple, pineapple and avocado concoctions.

Spirulina Powder

This deep-green powder is gathered from a small alga that grows in alkaline waters, and it is cultivated and harvested in hygienic tanks and ponds. It is considered a complete vegetable protein and is packed with trace minerals, cell salts and digestive enzymes. It is especially rich in chlorophyll, bringing you the highest benefits (of any plants) derived from photosynthesis—in the light of the sun!

One tablespoon of this concentrate contains 20 to 24 grams of high-quality protein (comparable to 80 grams of meat protein). Spirulina complements the flavors of avocado, pineapple, berries, coconut, apple, grape, tomato and carrot juices. You'll want to experiment with its taste. I recommend drinking it in the midmorning and midafternoon hours versus later at night, as it is so energy inducing.

Barley Green Powder and Wheatgrass Powder

These days, green-colored powders are cultivated from juices of sprouted barley and wheat seeds. Like spirulina, they are a goldmine of nutritional factors, including chlorophyll, minerals, enzymes. Barley green powder has a mellow sort of dynamism that is very tasty—especially in carrot juice. Wheatgrass powder is a bit grassier tasting but lends a fresh, light, earthy enrichment to the flavor of a vegetable cocktail.

Super Blue-Green Algae

Super Blue Green Algae,™ harvested from pristine Lake Klamath in Klamath Falls, Oregon, is one of the most dynamic 'super foods' on the planet. It is 67 percent protein (an alkaline plant source) and 97 percent absorbable in the human body. Containing vitamins, minerals, enzymes, co-enzymes, trace minerals, beta carotene, nucleic acids and useable carbohydrates such as glycogen, it nourishes the whole body. It detoxifies the body and builds strength where strength is needed!

(See *Directory of Ingredients* for sources of the above items.)

Liquids
Giving Luster

The ingredient that makes my bounty of Smoothies come alive with luster is *liquid*. Water, juices and milks made in nature's newest tradition add versatility and fun to the art of blending. Here is some "drink for thought" that encourages you to explore as many healthful options as you can.

Pure Water

Many things about the human body astonish me, including the fact that over half of it is made of water. Water is the powerful element that is needed to cleanse and regenerate our organs and cells as it guides the inflow of nutrients and the outflow of waste.

All fruits and vegetables provide water, yet additional water is usually need to spin them into smooth nectars.

I rely on spring water as well as water that comes out of a reverse osmosis purifying unit that is attached to the plumbing under my kitchen sink. There are many such purifiers available that will remove (or drastically cut down) the heavy metals, pesticides, chlorine, fluoride, asbestos, bacteria, parasites and other contaminants which threaten our municipal water supplies. It is probable that the

murky taste of such water can be disguised by recipe ingredients but very unlikely that the health problems associated with drinking it will go unnoticed for long.

We can gain a sense of cleaning up nature as well as the internal environment of our bodies when care is taken to prepare our food with pure water.

Fresh Pressed Juices

If you've never pressed a fruit or vegetable through a juice extractor, you won't want to postpone the thrill much longer!

When you can make a long, woody carrot disappear into a chute and have it reappear in just seconds as liquid orange in your glassware it's a lot like magic!

And when the precious nectar reaches the back of your throat you'll probably dream about every other fruit and vegetable tasting as sublime! You needn't be an avid juicer to accomplish the recipes in this book. Although, when and if you do manage to prepare nature's bounty in liquid fashion, you're bound to find the possibilities of their application exciting.

Since vegetable juices are a rare find at most regular stores (with the exception of tomato juices), the incentive is present to juice my own. I've found that peppers, cucumbers, zuchinni, tomatoes, etc. make a delicious unpasteurized version of "V8." Such a blend can then be tastefully texturized with ingredients such as avocado, corn (fresh or canned) and herbs. Carrot juice, nature's sweet and earthy vegetable, manages to enrich the color and flavor of pumpkin and squash-based Smoothies. Combining the juice with avocados is also nice when you can subtly spice them up with a hint of apple and/or pineapple juice. It is best if the ingredients don't compete for equal attention, however. As a general rule, it isn't advisable to mix vegetable and fruit juices since they require different digestive enzymes.

But you might occasionally find yourself making an exception or two for your tastebuds. I sometimes dilute fruit and vegetable juices (60 percent juice, 40 percent water) because they have such a high carbohydrate content. Consumed in excess, juices can overload the pancreas, kidneys and digestive "furnace" in general.

Because juices provide the biochemic make-up of a whole food, it is important to let them mix with the saliva (enzymes) for a few seconds before swallowing them. Unlike plain water, they require digestion. Combined with other ingredients, such as those in a thick blender drink, you are invited to savor them at a pace that's friendly to your body's needs.

Bottled Juices

Besides being convenient, bottled juices, particularly organically grown flavors, are flattering to the wide array of fresh fruits you might combine them with.

When using fresh fruit, juices can often be replaced by water in recipes, yet they simply offer to enhance your fun and creativity. Coconut juice blended with bananas and dates, for instance, is a real treat. Apple and "cranapple" juices are a delight blended with the same choice of fresh fruit, nuts, sweetener and spice. Most natural food grocery stores stock juices in flavors ranging from pear (it's mellow) and peach (fresh!) to cherry, pineapple and passion fruit. While it's easy to get into the rut of apple and orange juice, I find incentive for new recipes when I make a point of trying new juices.

Seasonal changes seem to offer the perfect opportunity for rotating choices. In the four-season climate where I live, I'm most inclined to reach for orange, peach, grapefruit, pineapple and passion fruit during the summer months. As autumn turns, I can't help but remember the harvest for apple, cranberry and pear juices. Refreshing cherry, grape and pear apple juices seem to me to have a cleansing and sunlit appeal during the spring.

For wintertime drinks, I rely less on fruit juices. Instead, I find seasonal dietary support in the soak-water from rehydrated dried fruit, as well as nutmilk, soymilk and grain milk. Of course, these natural "food" beverages can be enjoyed all year round.

Non-Dairy Milks

Nondairy milk products such as soymilk, nutmilk and rice milk, are wonderful alternatives to cow's milk and give Smoothies a richly satisfying taste and texture.

Unlike cow's milk which is high in cholesterol and fat (over half its calories come from fat), milks made from whole plant foods (such as soybeans, nuts, seeds and grain) are rich sources of vitamins, minerals, enzymes and healthful, unsaturated fatty acids.

The integrity of these elements are radically altered in the production of pasteurized and homogenized cow's milk.

Making the New Choice

It is estimated that 50 million people in the United States alone suffer from lactose intolerance, an inability to digest milk sugar. And millions more suffer from milk-related health conditions ranging from allergies to atherosclerosis.

Many health authorities believe these problems correlate with the problems of modern-day milk farming. Cows are exhausted by artificial breeding practices (conveniently inseminated by farmers) and given powerful growth hormones. Some animals graze on radioactive pasture and dine on not only alfalfa and hay, but also feathers, plastic and newspaper. Since diseases are prevalent on "factory" farms, drugs and antibiotics are routinely given.

Unfortunately, these factors end up in the inno-cent-looking white beverage that is sold to the public. A sensible and very creative solution to this dilemma is to make your own nondairy milks, or to purchase the ones that are now available at most natural food grocery stores and co-ops across the country.

At least a few brands of soymilk in appetizing flavors can be found, in cartons ranging from six ounces to a quart. Rice milk (amazake) is gaining popularity as well, in a few select flavors such as plain, fruit, vanilla, almond and mocha.

Nutmilk, another dairy substitute is a relative newcomer. I love making nutmilks from scratch at home and find pleasure in the variety that I can achieve using different nuts, seeds, spices, flavorings and unique fortifiers. Unlike the homemade preparation for soy and rice milks, which requires keeping a vigil over boiling beans or incubating rice grains, nutmilks can be made in only five minutes.

With the aid of a seed (coffee) grinder and blender, you can transform such ingredients as nuts, flaxseeds, lecithin granules, fresh and reconstituted fruits, wholesome sweeteners and water or diluted juices, into creamy, rich (yet nonfattening) drinks. They have a wonderfully healing effect on the whole body.

In my book, *Not Milk, NUTMILKS!*, I show you how you can create milks in as many as forty delightful flavors, and containing only 150 calories (approximately) per serving.

Discover Nutritional Support In Nut, Soy and Grain Milks

One of the things you'll appreciate about my nutmilk recipes, is that they offer an abundant sip of essential fatty acids. The body has trouble making these fatty acids (namely, omega 3 and 6) on its own. These elements offer to promote glandular hormones and boost the immune system, as well as police "bad fats" in the bloodstream. Fatty acids contribute to a supple, smooth complexion as well, and they work with vitamin D in the body, which assists in the utilization of calcium.

Allow me to introduce on the following page a basic introductory recipe for nutmilk as well as nutritional information about the values found in soy and grain milk.

Recipe for Nutmilk

⅓ c. raw nuts (your choice of almond, walnut, cashew, pecan, etc.

1 T. flaxseeds

1 t. lecithin granules

2-3 T. liquid sweetener (honey, maple syrup or rice syrup)

1 t. vanilla flavoring (adjust)

3 c. hot water

Preparing Nut And Seed Milks In Four Easy Steps

1. In a one- to two-quart saucepan, heat approximately four cups of pure water to desired temperature. Turn stove off and allow to sit while you prepare the other ingredients.

2. Select and gather refrigerated, fresh nuts and flaxseed. Place approximately one-fourth to one-third cup of nuts in the grinder. Cover to activate grinding blades. Press and release a few times to grind the seed/nut mix, which should resemble a fine powder-within about 15 to 20 seconds. Transfer the ground mixture to a blender. Add flaxseed to grinder, plus any remaining nuts and repeat process. Transfer to your blender.

3. To your blender, add lecithin granules, fortifiers, a sweetener of your choice, flavoring extract, and any fresh or reconstituted fruit. Then add one-half to three-fourths cup of the warm or hot water (from your stove top) and blend on medium speed to a smooth, pudding-like puree. Add the remaining water suggested in the recipe and reblend on high speed until creamy.

Use approximately three cups water per recipe for extra-creamy nutmilks and use as much as one-half to three-fourths cup more for a thinner version. Amounts are suggested in the recipes; you may choose to vary them, as well as the water (or juice) temperature.

4. Pour the contents of the blender through a fine mesh strainer into a bowl or pitcher. Use a spoon to stir the milk while you pour, since it will be slightly too rich to flow through the strainer without a bit of mashing. Serve immediately or bottle and refrigerate for up to 72 hours.

Rice Milk (Amazake)

Amazake is a light, refreshing drink with incredible, natural sweetness. It is made from cultured, whole-grain brown rice. Koji (pronounced Ko-gee), a fermented rice, is added to cooked rice, causing an enzyme action to break down its starches. As the mixture incubates, its sweetness develops, creating a nectar that resembles milk in appearance.

You might use only a few ounces of this milk to add flavor and nutrition to Smoothies featuring nuts, grains and fruits. Amazake's appeal becomes more luxurious in the process. An eight-ounce serving of plain Amazake contains 200 calories by itself. Combined with other food values, you can expect a healthy calorie drink that will replenish you after exercise or workouts! Amazake is also available as a frozen dessert cream and gives Smoothies a frosty, dessert-like appeal.

Rice Dream is a tradename used by one producer of amazake, both liquid and frozen.

Soymilk

Commercially prepared soymilk is a nutritional and good-tasting beverage made from organic soybeans, as well as cereal extracts and natural flavorings. Malted soymilks, which have an extra-creamy consistency, often have a measure of oil added to them as well. An eight-ounce glass of this milk contains about nine grams of protein, slightly more than is found in the same amount of cow's milk.

Soymilk can be used in conjunction with other nondairy milks, and is also available in frozen dessert-cream consistency.

Pure Coconut Milk

Pure coconut milk adds body and flavor to Smoothies, as well as nutritional value. It has a rich mineral content and is high in vitamins A and B, protein and iodine. An all-natural (preservative-free) coconut milk I stock in my pantry is a brand inported from Malaysia. It's called Epicurean International. See product directory at the end of this book for information on the availability of this product in your area.

Part Three

Your

Culinary Helpers

There are many occasions when culinary helpers, such as juicers, blenders and seed grinders, can be used in a complementary way to make food fibers amenable to one another.

You'll want to establish a user-friendly acquaintance with these appliances as you explore the exciting new recipe options they can help you create.

Juicers

There are many different manufacturers and styles of juicers, and it is best to study them before purchasing. You might ask your local health food store for consumer information from the companies that distribute them. A good juicer should last a lifetime with proper care. If you've been inclined to participate in a whole foods lifestyle as long as I, you may have already experimented with more than one unit! The units I am familiar with include Champion, Phoenix, Acme, Miracle, Omega and Juiceman. The Champion juicer is a sleek machine with a long snout, and flexible in the sense that it can be used to make ice cream (from frozen bananas) as well as nutbutters. The juice it makes needs to be strained, as there is a fine, pulpy taste to it.

Centrifugal juicers such as the Acme, Phoenix, Juiceman, Miracle and Omega are efficient units that don't take up a lot of space on your kitchen countertop. The Acme has a pulp basket in its interior core which holds the pulp from making a quart of juice. It needs to be emptied before a new quart can be made. The other models have pulp ejectors which make the task of clearing away pulp slightly more efficient.

The juice made by these machines may or may not need straining.

Juices are best when drunk immediately after pressing them. However, some sit fairly well in the refrigerator for 24 hours.

Blenders

Blenders are so useful, I can't imagine being without one. Of course, Smoothies necessitate a blender. Glass and stainless steel blenders are available at most houseware departments, and I recommend them instead of plastic. Since plastic is synthetic material, and since hot or near boiling water is sometimes added to recipes, stainless steel makes better sense. Always follow the operating instructions that accompany your blender. Use care not to stick utensils into a food blend while the machine is on. Stop the machine and stir any ingredients before reblending. When working with a thick mixture of ingredients, it is helpful to pour a portion of the liquid recommended in the recipe directly into the bottom of the blender before adding the recipe ingredients. This jumpstarts the blending process.

Grinders

They are called nut, seed, herb, spice or coffee bean grinders, and they are unequivocally one of the best small investments I've ever made in an electric kitchen appliance. The cap on this compact grinding unit lifts off so that you can add as much as one-third cup of dry food. The stainless steel rotary blades are activated by pushing down on the cap for several seconds. Repeating the process may be necessary to pulverize the grinder's contents.

Grinders can do what blenders can't when it comes to tiny seeds, such as flaxseed, sesame or chia seeds. I use them in the first step of nutmilk preparation—and they are great for efficiency. Some brands of grinders include Moulinex, Krups and Oster. They are available at houseware and small electrical appliance departments everywhere.

Recipe Rainbow

Taste the Nectar of Life!

Smoothies in Earth Tones of Red

Apple Berry Rhubarb

A tangy and light, yet sumptuous summer garden drink
that is ruby red!

1 c. rehydrated apples
1 c. frozen rhubarb chunks
½-¾ c. fresh or frozen strawberries
2 T. honey
1½ c. apple or pear juice
½ c. water (adjust)

To create: Rehydrate dried apples (as indicated on page 55). Add apple or pear juice to the blender, along with apples, berries, rhubarb and sweetener. Blenderize until smooth.

Serves: 2-4

Cranapple Pear

Rehydrated, dried pears add the silky body to this zesty
pair of flavors.

1 c. rehydrated pears
2 medium, red apples (sliced)
⅛ t. cinnamon powder
1-2 T. honey or rice syrup
1½ c. cranberry juice blend (I used Knudsen brand)
½ c. water (or as desired)

To create: Rehydrate dried pears (as indicated on page 55). Lightly peel apple. Pour water and cranberry juice into blender. Add sliced apples, spices and sweetener. Blend on medium-high speed until smooth.

Serves 2-4

Spicy Apple Tree

A smooth, yet fibrous and fruity nectar.

2 fresh apples
1 medium-small, ripe banana
¼ c. dark raisins, soaked
¼ t. peanut butter
1 T. honey or Sucanat
pinch of cinnamon and/or coriander powder
1 c. water
3-4 ice cubes (opt.)

To create: Peel banana and lightly peel apples before slicing into small pieces. Combine in the blender with remaining ingredients. Blend until smooth. Add ice if desired and reblend.

Serves 2-4

Apple Raisin Lassi

Rehydrated apples team up with barley, raisins and spices for an incredibly nourishing treat.

1 c. dried apples, soaked
¾ c. pearled barley, cooked
¼ c. raisins, soaked
⅛ t. cardamom powder
¼ t. cinnamon
1 t. fresh lemon juice
¼ t. vanilla flavoring
¾ c. malted almond soymilk
½-¾ c. malted vanilla soymilk

To create: Have barley ready beforehand. Rehydrate fruit as indicated on page 55-56. Add liquids and spices to your blender along with soaked fruits and barley. Blend on high speed until smooth.

Serves 4.

Pineapple Zest

Sweet, ripe pineapple, tangy cranberries, and apple pectin sing in harmony in this light, pink-red drink.

¼-⅓ c. rehydrated cranberries

1 c. fresh pineapple chunks

1 medium-large, fresh, red-skinned apple—lightly peeled

1-2 T. orange juice concentrate (or ¼ t. orange flavoring)

⅛-¼ c. fresh, raw almonds (opt.)

1-2 T. honey

1 c. apple juice

½ c. pear juice or water

To create: Rehydrate dried cranberries (as indicated on page 55). Combine with pineapple, fresh apples and juices in the blender. Puree smooth. If you choose to add nuts, grind to a fine powder, using an electric seed grinder.

Serves 4

Cherry Plum Blossom

*Blush with life when you sip on the deep, cherry-red color
of this nectar. It's an ideal spring cleanser and mineral
fortifier.*

1 golden-skinned apple
4 ripe plums
¾-1 c. frozen, pitted cherries
2 T. honey
½-1 c. water (adjust)
¼ c. fresh raw almonds (opt.)
1 t. fresh lemon juice (opt.) or pinch of cloves

To create: Lightly peel and slice apple and plums.
Combine with cherries, sweetener, water and honey
in the blender. Puree smooth. Add almonds or a
drop of almond extract if desired. Or, try the other
optional suggestions and reblend.

Serves 3

Satin Cherry

*Cooked in water or a light fruit juice, tapioca lends silky,
nourishing sensations to the fruit in this light nectar.*

1 c. frozen, pitted cherries
½ c. frozen banana (opt.) or substitute with fresh,
    peeled pear
1-1½ c. dairy-free tapioca (cooked and chilled)
3 T. honey (adjust)
1½ c. apple and/or pear juice
½ t. lemon juice (opt.)

To create: A day ahead, prepare tapioca, according
to instructions on page 74. Add to blender, along
with cherries, bananas, sweetener and juices. Adjust
liquids with precision to create a silky versus
slippery texture. Serve in sleek glass tumblers.

Serves 3-4

Fresh Cactus Pear

*Pomegranate and melon are the sweet, yet tangy flavors
that come to mind when I sip on this simple concoction
of prickly pears and juice. Pucker your lips for its
bright, fuchsia-pink color.*

3 prickly pears
1½ c. apple juice or pear juice

To create: Peel ripened prickly pears and slice into blender. Add juice(s) and blend. Strain before drinking, since prickly pears have seeds.

Serves 2

Piña Pear

*Rehydrated, dried pears give this Smoothie a deep-reddish,
pear-flecked color that lends tasty fiber to the diet.*

1 c. rehydrated pears
1-2 T. fresh lemon juice
2 t. orange juice concentrate
½ c. each pear juice and piña colada juice
1 c. apple juice

To create: Rehydrate dried, unsulphured pears as indicated on page 55. Combine softened fruit with juices in your blender and puree smooth.

Serves 2

Figgy Cranapple Nut

*If you consider yourself a "healthy gourmet" you'll
appreciate the richly satisfying tastes and nutritional
texture of this Smoothie.*

⅛-¼ c. rehydrated cranberries
⅓-⅔ c. Calymirna figs
⅓ c. fresh almonds (or walnuts)
1-2 T. orange juice concentrate
1 T. honey or Sucanat
2 c. apple juice (adjust as desired)

To create: Slice figs and rehydrate as indicated on page 55. Do the same with the dried cranberries.

Grind refrigerated, fresh nuts into powder, using an electric seed grinder. Add 1 c. apple juice to blender before adding soft figs, cranberries, nutmeal, orange juice and sweetener. Begin blending process, adding remaining juice as needed. Stop blender to stir ingredients if necessary. Resume blending until ingredients are smooth.

Serves 2-4

Spicy Raspberry Rainbow

*Three fruits coupled with a hint of ginger and coconut
    lend this drink a tropical appeal. Decorate its luscious
    raspberry color with a mint leaf.*

1 c. frozen raspberries
1 ripe banana
2 medium-size, ripe peaches
½-1 t. fresh ginger
1 c. coconut-fruit blend juice
1 T. sweetener (opt.)

To create: Peel and grate a tad of ginger. Peel fresh peaches and slice. Combine with raspberries, bananas and coconut juice in blender and puree smooth. Drink immediately.

Serves 4

Raspberry Revel

*Enjoy the soft, mauve raspberry hue of this Smoothie
while discovering the healthy magic it spins from
raspberries and fruity chocolate sauce.*

1½ frozen bananas
¾ c. raspberries (fresh or frozen)
½ c. vanilla frozen amazake (see p. 103)
1-3 t. chocolate fruit sauce (I used Chocolate
Mountain brand)
1 t. slippery elm powder (opt.)
¼ c. fresh, raw, ground almonds (opt.)
½+ c. water (as needed or desired, to blend)

To create: Break frosty bananas into small chunks.
Add approximately (½+ c.) water to the blender,
followed by frozen amazake, chocolate sauce, elm
powder and nuts. Begin blending process. As the
texture becomes smooth, add bananas and raspberries. Continue blending, adding more water only if
needed. Puree on high speed until thick and creamy.

Note: Chocolate Mountain chocolate sauce contains
unsweetened Dutch cocoa and concentrated fruit
juices such as pear, peach and pineapple. It is
available at many fine health food stores.

Serves 2-3

Raspberry Ruffle

*"Light and luminescent" might best describe this sweet
and tangy raspberry sensation.*

1 c. frozen raspberries
1½ c. dairy-free tapioca (cooked and chilled)
⅛ c. fresh lemon juice
3½ T. honey
¼ t. each orange and coconut flavoring
½+ c. water and/or several ice cubes
    (sparkling water could be used)

To create: A day ahead, cook tapioca according to
instructions on page 74. Add tapioca to blender,
along with raspberries, lemon juice, sweetener,
flavoring extracts and water. Adjust water with
precision, to create a silky versus slippery texture.
Serve in a sleek glass tumbler.

Serves 3

Raspberry Tart Softie

*This beautiful, berry-colored nectar has the tang of a
  fruity soda. The fact that it's so simple to make adds to
  the joy of sipping it.*

1-1½ c. fresh, ripe papaya (about 1½ medium-size
  papaya fruit)
½-¾ c. frozen raspberries
½ c. lemon- or vanilla-flavored frozen amazake
  (see p. 103)
2 T. honey (adjust)

To create: Cut open and peel skin from papaya,
discarding any seeds from the portion to be used.
Combine with raspberries, frozen amazake, and
sweetener in blender. Puree smooth.

Serves 2-3

Strawberry Strudel

*Here's a delectable strawberry Smoothie with the appeal of
  a dessert. Serve warm or chilled, for breakfasts or
  snacks.*

¾ c. rehyrated apples
1 c. strawberries (fresh or frozen)
1-2 T. rice syrup or honey
6-10 oz. malted vanilla soymilk
2-4 T. fresh granola (opt.); I used oat granola with
  dried strawberry bits.

To create: Rehydrate dried apples as indicated on
page 55. Add soymilk to blender, along with
rehydrated fruit, strawberries and sweetener. Blend
until smooth and creamy. Taste to see if granola is
desired. Reblend as necessary.

Serves 2-3

Tropical Strawberry

In the summer, when bowls and Tupperware containers
are filled with different fruits, try combining this
pretty, soft earthen rainbow of flavors.

1 c. frozen strawberries
½ c. pineapple
⅓-½ c. ripe papaya
1 small peach
½ fresh, ripe avocado
½ c. apple juice
½ + c. piña colada juice
¼ t. coconut flavoring (opt.)
1 t. lime juice (opt.)

To create: Peel, seed and slice pineapple, papaya, peach and avocado. Combine with strawberries, juices and flavoring in the blender. Puree until smooth.

Serves 2-3

Strawberry Girl

When the strawberry patch calls you outside to "play,"
bring nature's plump, heart-shaped fruits home for this
simple and sweet favorite.

2½ c. strawberries—fresh or frozen
2 c. almond nutmilk or malted vanilla soymilk
ice (opt.); or ½ c. frozen banana
2+ T. honey

To create: Prepare nutmilk (see page 102). Combine with strawberries in the blender and puree smooth. Add ice or a small bit of frozen banana and reblend until smooth and creamy.

Serves 2

Tangy Tomato Artichoke

Tangy and refreshing, this "cream-of-tomato soup cocktail" nicely curbs the appetite before the dinner hour.

¼ c. marinated artichoke hearts
1 medium-small celery stalk
½ fresh lemon
1 T. Parmesan cheese (opt.)
1+ c. tomato juice
½ c. water
ice cubes
parsley or celery leaf garnish

To create: Slice artichoke hearts and the celery. Combine with fresh-squeezed lemon juice, Parmesan, tomato juice and water in the blender. Puree smooth. For extra refreshing appeal, add ice cubes and reblend. Serve in cocktail glasses with garnish.

Serves 2

Earthy Garden Tomato

Hearty enough to be considered a mini-meal in itself,
you might serve this Smoothie in a small tumbler or
soup cup with a cracker on the side.

4 c. tomato juice
1-2 small patty-pan squash
1 green scallion
½ fresh, ripe avocado (peeled and pitted)
¼ c. tofu
⅛ c. alfalfa sprouts (opt.)
1 T. Bragg's Liquid Amino Bouillon
dash of garlic and onion powder
2-3 ice cubes (opt.)

To create: Slice patty-pan squash, green scallion, avocado and tofu. Combine in the blender with tomato juice, bouillon, herbs, and sprouts if desired. Blend smooth. Add ice cubes and reblend. Garnish with parsley sprig or cherry tomato halves. Drink immediately.

Serves 4

Velvet Tomato

Here's a delicious and smooth drink that is rich in calcium, enzymes and vitamins.

2 c. tomato juice
1 t. miso paste
1 t. sesame tahini
2 t. almond butter
1+ T. nutritional yeast powder
dash onion powder
1 t. spirulina powder (opt.)

To create: Blend all ingredients smooth in your blender.

Serves 2

Variation: Omit miso and nut butter. Flavor with soya amino bouillon and a delicate sprinkle of herbs such as garlic, basil, onion and red pepper powders. Try a squirt of lemon juice or dulse flakes as well.

Gazpacho Tang

*The vegetables sparkle in this easy-to-make drink
   that whets the appetite.*

1 ripe tomato
½ medium-large cucumber
1 green scallion
¼ c. green bell pepper
1 T. olive oil
2-3 t. red wine vinegar
½ t. chili powder
¼ t. onion powder
½ t. Spike herbal seasoner
1 tiny clove of garlic (or dash of garlic powder)
1+ c. tomato juice (adjust as desired)
¼-½ c. sparkling mineral water (opt.)

To create: Peel tomato and cucumber before slicing, along with the scallion and bell pepper. Combine with the remaining ingredients in the blender and puree smooth. Serve in a sleek tumbler and garnish with lemon twist or parsley. Drink immediately.

Serves 3-4

Summer Salsa Combo

*This easy-to-whip-up cocktail offers another opportunity
to "drink your vegetables."*

2½-3 c. tomato juice
2-3 T. green bell pepper
¼ c. corn kernels
¼ c. zucchini
1 green scallion
1-2 t. cilantro leaf
2 T. fresh, ripe avocado (peeled and pitted)
Spike herbal seasoner to taste
¼ t. Mexican seasoning
2 ice cubes (opt.)

To create: Slice the bell pepper, zucchini, scallion
and avocado. Combine in the blender with tomato
juice, corn, cilantro and seasoners. Blend until
smooth. Drink immediately.

Serves 2-3

Tangy Tomato Sauerkraut

*Chock full of enzymes, this tangy drink promotes the
healthy intestinal flora that encourages good digestion.*

2 c. tomato juice
½ c. sauerkraut (juice or kraut)
1 T. bouillon
2 t. yeast and a dash of bacon yeast powder
1 t. cashew butter (opt.)
garnish: parsley/dulse flakes

To create: Combine all ingredients in blender and
puree smooth.

Serves 2

Pineapple Rose

"Where's the beet?" you might ask. Iron and potassium
never tasted so good!

2 c. pineapple chunks
1½ c. apple juice (adjust)
3-6 T. beet juice
⅛ t. coconut flavoring (opt.); ½ c. coconut milk
could also substitute one part of apple juice.

To create: Rely on leftover beet juice to make this drink easily. Peel and slice pineapple. Combine with juices in blender and puree smooth.

Serves 2

Smoothies in Earth Tones of Orange

Sweet Cinnamon Pumpkin Vine

This creamy, sweetly spiced sensation possesses a deep, golden yellow ochre color that exudes beta carotene, protein and minerals!

1⅔ c. pumpkin (I used canned Festal brand)
1 T. brown rice syrup
2 T. Sucanat
⅛-¼ c. fresh, raw organic pumpkin seeds
½ t. pumpkin pie spice (contains cinnamon, ginger, cloves and nutmeg)
1+ c. vanilla soymilk (regular or creamy malted)
2-3 ice cubes; opt.
1 t. vanilla flavoring
¼ c. soaked raisins (see pp. 55,56)

To create: Grind pumpkin seeds to a fine meal, using an electric seed grinder. Combine soymilk, spices, sweeteners, seeds and pumpkin in your blender. Puree until smooth. Add ice if desired, and reblend. Raisins add a depth of flavor.

Note: Be sure to use unsprayed organic pumpkin seeds, as some varieties contain the unpleasant taste of pesticides.

Serves 2-4

Heavenly Apricot Yam

This Smoothie bursts with sweet, tangy flavor and food value.

2 medium-large sweet potatoes (about 2½ c.)
⅓ c. dried unsulphured apricots, soaked
3 T. maple syrup
1 c. orange juice.
2 c. liquid (water, malted vanilla soymilk or coconut milk)

To create: In advance, bake sweet potatoes until tender (as indicated on page 67). Rehydrate apricots as indicated on page 55. Peel skins from potatoes and slice into chunks. Add water and orange juice to blender. Add sweet potatoes and syrup. Blend on medium speed to begin with, then on high-speed until creamy consistency is reached.

Serves 4.

Creamy Butterscotch Yam

If you like butterscotch pudding, you'll love this scrumptious and drinkable vitamin-rich rendition of it. Serve up in an elegant tumbler or dessert dish and spoon or sip to your spleen's content!

2 medium-size sweet potatoes (about 2 c.)
1+ T. brown rice syrup
1 T. Sucanat
1 t. vanilla flavoring
¼-½ t. butterscotch flavoring
2-2½ c. water (or malted vanilla soy milk)
2 ice cubes (opt.)
2 t. sesame tahini

To create: In advance, bake sweet potatoes until tender as indicated on page 67. Let cool in refrigerator. Peel skins from potatoes and slice into small chunks. Add sweet potatoes to blender along with water, tahini, sweeteners and flavorings. Begin blending. After several seconds of blending, stop the unit and mix the ingredients, if necessary, using a long utensil. Reblend to a creamy consistency. Serve warm or chilled.

Serves 3-4.

Malaysian Pineapple Sweet Potato

*Sweet potatoes make a luscious statement in this
easy-to-prepare, easy-to-digest Smoothie that energizes
the body with the "orange vibration."*

2 medium-size sweet potatoes (about 2 c.)
1½ c. pure coconut milk
1-2 T. pineapple orange juice concentrate
½ c. water (adjust)

To create: In advance, bake sweet potatoes until
tender (as indicated on page 67). Let cool in
refrigerator. Peel skins from potatoes and slice into
small chunks. Combine in your blender with coconut
milk and pineapple orange concentrate. Puree
smooth. Serve chilled.

Serves 2-4

*Note—See *Liquids Giving Luster* for availability of
coconut milk

Tropical Banana Sweet Potato

Enjoy beta carotine and minerals, in delicious supply!

2 medium-size sweet potatoes (about 2 c.)
½ c. fresh, ripe banana
2 T. syrup (rice, maple or barley malt)
2 c. rice milk or coconut milk

To create: Bake sweet potatoes as indicated on page
67. Let cool in refrigerator. Peel skins from potatoes and
slice into blender. Add banana, sweeteners and liquids.
Blend on high speed until creamy, adjusting liquid as
needed.

Serves 4.

Candied Yam Softie

*Imagine the creamy texture of yogurt mixed with
orange juice when you envision this drink.
Made with high- quality organic sweet potatoes, it
promises to be a bright and pure orange color with a
light, refreshing taste.*

3 medium-size sweet potatoes (yams);
       about 2½+ c.
⅛ c. fresh raw cashews
2 T. maple syrup
¼ t. orange flavoring
2½-3 c. water
2 ice cubes (opt.)

To create: In advance, bake sweet potatoes until
tender (as indicated on page 67). Let cool in the
refrigerator. Peel skins from potatoes and slice into
small chunks. Pour water into blender and add sweet
potatoes, cashew meal, sweetener and flavoring.
Blend until smooth and creamy. Serve chilled.

Note: Use an electric seed grinder to prepare
cashew meal.

Serves 4

Toasted Swiss Almond Carrot

Craving something delicious, yet nutritious? Not even an ice cream vendor could compete with this pretty salmon-colored treat.

1 c. fresh carrot juice
2 c. Swiss almond, frozen amazake (see p. 103)
1 T. Cafix cereal-grain beverage powder
1 t. slippery elm powder

To create: Press carrots (4-5) through a juice extractor. Put juice in your blender along with the frozen amazake, Cafix and slippery elm powder. For a thicker version of this drink, you might consider adding ¼ c. of cooked pearled barley. If so, blend the barley into a creamy pudding first, using part of the carrot juice.

Note: You could replace Swiss almond frozen amazake with plain vanilla, then prepare you own almond meal using an electric seed grinder.

Serves 2-3

Coconut Carrot Blossom

Don't just 'eat' your carrots, 'drink' them!

1½-2 c. carrots, steamed tender
½ t. cinnamon
pinch of ginger, optional
pinch of nutmeg, optional
¾-1 c. malted vanilla soymilk
1 c. water (adjust as desired) or coconut milk

To create: Peel carrots, slice into small chunks and steam over the stove until tender, but still bright in color. Add to blender with spices and liquids. Blend on high speed until smooth. Chill in refrigerator.

Serves 4.

Enriched Carrot Nugget

The vivid, earthy orange colors in carrots and pumpkin
combine in this naturally sweet carbo-enriched drink.

1 c. carrot juice, chilled

1⅔ c. pumpkin (I used canned Festal brand)

1-2 T. honey (or try a dash or two of barley malt
sweetener powder*)

⅓ c. fresh-ground almond meal

⅛ t. cinnamon

pinch of nutmeg

½ t. vanilla flavoring (adjust)

¼-½ c. water;

2 ice cubes (opt.)

To create: In advance, juice carrots (4-6) and chill juice in the refrigerator (or use freshly made juice at room temperature). Combine juice, pumpkin, sweeteners, almond meal, spices and flavoring in the blender. Blend until smooth and creamy. Add additional water or ice cubes if desired and reblend.

Serves 2-3

* See *Wholesome Sweeteners.*

Sunflower Squash Blossom

*Earthy buttercup or acorn squash blossom with flavor
when blended with spices and sweet, non-dairy milk in
this full-bodied drink. Try it warmed, for seasonal
enjoyment, in the autumn and winter.*

1½+ c. squash (cooked puree)
1 T. almond butter
2 T. fresh, raw sunflower seeds
1 T. Sucanat sweetener (use extra if desired)
½-1 t. vanilla flavoring
½ t. cinnamon
¼ t. ginger (adjust as desired)
nutmeg (a pinch)
½ c. plain Amazake rice milk (or vanilla malted
    soymilk)
1 c. water (adjust)
⅛-¼ c. soaked raisins

To create: Bake squash in the oven until tender (see
instructions in vegetable section). Discard the green
shell around the portion of squash you'll use. Mash
or slice into smallish chunks. Grind sunflower seeds
to a fine meal, using an electric seed grinder. Add
water to your blender, followed by squash, almond
butter, seed meal, sweeteners, spices and "milk."
Begin blending process. Stop blender as needed to
facilitate the mixing of ingredients. Reblend on high
speed until smooth and creamy. Soaked raisins add a
sweet depth of flavor.

Serves 2-3

Chilled variation. Omit nut butter and seeds.
Substitute Sucanat with maple syrup to taste. Adjust
spices, adding allspice to ginger-nutmeg blend.

Malted Carrot and Molasses

"Mmmm, this stuff is yummy!" said my son when
I served it to him for an after-school winter snack.
Let your juicer grind carrots in a flash. Then, add the
finishing touches: calcium, iron, protein and fiber.
Serve warm or chilled.

½-¾ c. carrot juice
1 c. cooked, pearled barley
1-2 T. carob molasses syrup
1½ T. sesame tahini
2 T. Sucanat (or barley malt sweetener powder to
    taste)
1 t. vanilla flavoring
¾ c. vanilla-flavored rice milk (or malted soymilk)
¼-½ c. water (adjust)
¼ t. butterscotch flavoring (opt.)

To create: Have cooked barley ready beforehand, as
well as fresh-pressed carrot juice. Pour carrot juice
into blender with sweeteners, sesame tahini and
flavorings. Add barley, and puree smooth, like
pudding. Slowly add choice of milk and/or water
while the blender is running. Cover blender top and
resume blending on high speed until creamy.

Serves 2-4

Papaya Sunglow

*Here's a luscious, golden sip of the Hawaiian Islands,
that is rich in vitamin C, potassium and folacin.*

1 c. fresh, ripe papaya
½-1 c. frozen banana
1-2 T. honey or rice syrup
¼ t. each lemon and coconut flavorings
½ c. orange juice
½ c. papaya juice
½ c. vanilla frozen amazake (see p. 103)
½ c. water

To create: Cut open, peel and slice ripe orange papaya, discarding seeds from suggested portion. Break banana into smallish segments and combine with papaya, flavorings, sweetener, juice, frozen amazake and water in blender. Puree until smooth.

Serves 3

Papaya Sunset

*Taste the richness of a sunset in this carob and date-sweetened
nectar.*

2 fresh, ripe papaya
⅓ c. dates, soaked
1 T. carob powder
2 T. honey
1 c. malted vanilla soymilk

To create: Soak dates as indicated on pate 55. Combine all ingredients in blender and puree smooth.

Serves 3.

Apricot Almond Orange

The speckled texture of apricots speaks of nutritional authenticity in this Smoothie which is bursting with fiber, flavor and golden (yellow ochre) sunshine.

½ c. dried, unsulphured apricots; plus soak liquid as needed
1-2 T. fresh coconut flakes
¼ c. fresh, raw almonds
1-2 T. rice syrup
1⅓ c. orange juice; adjust
pinch nutmeg (opt.)
2 ice cubes (opt.)

To create: Using a jar, soak apricots overnight in water or apple/orange juice, as indicated on page 55. Grind coconut flakes into a fine meal, using an electric seed grinder. Grind almonds in the same fashion. Pour juice into blender and add apricots, nuts, coconut, rice syrup and spice. Blend until smooth and creamy. Add ice if desired and reblend.

Serves 2

Pearly Mandarin Apricot

⅔-¾ c. pearled barley, cooked tender
½ c. soaked apricots (plus ⅔ c. soak water)
1 T. Sucanat
2 T. honey
½ t. orange flavoring
¾ c. malted almond soymilk
½ c. water

To create: Have barley ready. Soak dried apricots. Combine all ingredients in blender. Blend on high speed until smooth.

Serves 3.

Orange Fruit Grove

A familiar, yet new twist of ingredients blend a sunny
flavor that will wake your taste buds.

2 c. orange juice
1 banana, frozen
½ c. golden raisins
½ c. frozen amazake (see p. 103)
¼ t. coconut flavor

To create: In advance, peel fresh, ripe banana and freeze until hard. Rehydrate raisins as indicated on page 55. Break bananas into small segments and combine with raisins, flavoring and orange juice in your blender. Puree smooth.

Note: Vanilla or lemon flavor frozen amazake can be used.

Serves 2

Melon Mint

Here's to beautiful summer mornings when you need a
refresher before getting started on any routines.

4 c. ripe cantaloupe
1-2 T. orange juice concentrate
3-4 fresh mint sprigs
½ c. water or coconut- fruit juice blend

To create: Cut open, peel and slice melon, discarding seeds from usable portion. Add to blender with remaining ingredients and puree smooth.

Serves 2

Calming Cantaloupe

This taste-pleasing, beige melon-colored nectar is soft and soothing. Yet, its natural sugars supply the body with energy-enhancing balance.

2 c. ripe cantaloupe
1 small, frozen banana
⅛-¼ c. rehydrated pitted dates
¼ t. coconut flavoring
1 c. water (or substitute with part coconut-fruit juice or coconut milk)

To create: In advance, peel fresh, ripe banana and freeze until hard. Rehydrate dates in water or coconut juice as indicated on page 55. Cut open and peel cantaloupe, discarding any seeds from the suggested portion. Slice into small chunks and add to blender with frozen fruit, dates, coconut flavoring and water. Blend until smooth. Drink immediately.

Serves 4

'Fruity Vegetable' Smoothie

Perfect for autumn sipping! And easy—if you have some leftover barley and squash to use up.

1 c. winter squash, cooked
½ c. mixture of raisins and dried apples (rehydrated)
⅓ c. pearled barley, cooked tender
2 T. Sucanat
1 T. rice syrup or maple syrup
¼ t. cinnamon powder
1 t. vanilla flavoring
¾ c. malted vanilla soymilk
1 c. water (adjust as desired)

To create: Have barley and squash ready beforehand. Rehydrate dried apples and raisins as indicated on page 55. Pour liquids into blender. Add spices, sweeteners and all remaining ingredients. Blend smooth.

Serves 3-4.

Tropical Papaya Cashew

Here's a sure-fire way to meet your body's need for vitamin A and digestive enzymes.

1-1½ c. fresh, ripe papaya
½ c. fresh, raw cashews
⅛ c. fresh, shredded coconut
1 t. orange or coconut flavoring
2 T. honey
½-1 c. water (adjust)

To create: Cut open and peel papaya, discarding any seeds from the usable portion suggested. Slice fruit and combine with coconut, nut meal, flavoring, sweetener and water. Puree until smooth.

Serves 2-3

Velvet Papaya Frappé

Here's a variation of "Tropical Papaya." When you
feature papaya with other ingredients, you can be sure
the papane enzymes will lend it digestive power.

1½ c. fresh, ripe papaya
⅛-¼ c. dates or strawberries
1-2 T. orange juice concentrate
1 t. coconut flavoring
1-2 T. honey
½ c. malted vanilla soymilk
water (as desired)

To create: Peel and slice papaya, discarding any seeds from suggested portion. Rehydrate dates. Combine all ingredients in your blender and puree smooth.

Serves 2

Tropical Squash

1½ bananas, peeled and sliced
½ c. winter squash (cooked 'leftovers')
2 T. Sucanat
1 c. nondairy vanilla-flavored ice cream

To create: Blend all ingredients in blender, using water as needed to create a smooth consistency.

Sparkling Crème de Mango

*Summer is the right time to serve this sparkling
refreshment that all ages will love.*

1-1½ c. fresh, ripe mango or papaya
½-¾ c. lemon-flavored frozen amazake (see p. 103)
½ c. diluted orange juice concentrate (thick juice)
1 T. honey
¾ c. water
¼ c. sparking water (opt.)

To create: Peel and cut open mango or papaya,
discarding any seeds from the usable portion suggested. Slice fruit, and combine with remaining
ingredients in blender. Puree smooth.

Serves 2

Smoothies in Earth Tones
of Yellow and Cream

Peachy Piña Colada

This creamy, light-yellow smoothie is bursting with pure fruit flavor, vitamins, minerals and fiber.

1 medium-size fresh peach
1 c. fresh pineapple
¼ c. soaked golden raisins
1 small, frozen banana
1 c. piña colada juice (I use Summer Song brand)
½-1 c. water

To create: Rehydrate raisins (see page 55). Peel and slice peach and pineapple. Break frozen banana into small chunks. Combine juices and water with fruit in your blender and puree on high speed until smooth and creamy.

Serves 3-4

Pineapple Cashew Paradise

*Because pineapple aids digestion and helps rid the body
of excess weight, it combines well with foods rich in
fatty acids, such as coconut and cashews.*

2 c. fresh pineapple
1 small, frozen banana (opt).
⅛-¼ c. fresh, raw cashews
⅛-¼ c. dates (pitted)
1½ c. coconut milk (I used pure coconut milk)

To create: Peel pineapple and slice into small chunks. Reconstitute dates as indicated on page 55. Grind fresh nuts to a fine meal, using an electric seed grinder. Break banana into small pieces. Combine all ingredients in your blender with coconut milk and puree on high speed until smooth.

Note: See *Liquids Giving Luster* (page 95) for availability of coconut milk.

Serves 2

Peach and Almond Tree

*Here's a velvety fruit nectar that's light, yet nourishing.
Try it with a high-fiber cookie or snack bar.*

4 medium-size peaches
6 oz. malted vanilla soymilk (or almond nutmilk)
⅛-¼ t. almond flavoring (or vanilla)

To create: Simply peel ripe peaches and slice into the blender. Blend with soymilk and flavoring until smooth.

If you have only soymilk available, you could add a touch of liquid sweetener and a teaspoon of oil to add creaminess.

Serves 2-4

Almond Soy Rice Nog

You might think of this as a fancy banana-flavored eggnog (sans the egg and dairy). Even kids like this version of "any day is a holiday ..."

1½ c. Amazake rice milk (two 6 oz. cartons, original flavor)
¾ c. malted almond soymilk (or almond nutmilk)
1 small, ripe banana (about ½ c.)
½ t. nutmeg (adjust as desired)
1 t. vanilla flavoring
pinch of sea salt and turmeric
pinch of cardamom powder (opt.)

To create: See *Liquids Giving Luster* (page 95) for preparation of nondairy options. Combine banana, flavoring, spices and nondairy milk in your blender. Puree smooth.

Note: Almond butter could be used, along with plain soymilk, to create your own homemade version.

Serves 2-3

Frosty Banana Elm and Currant

This is a luscious and zesty treat that you might never guess is fortified with enzymes, essential fatty acids and minerals!

2 frozen bananas
½ c. currants and/or raisins
¼-⅓ c. fresh walnuts
1 T. fresh flaxseed
2 t. slippery elm powder
1-1½ c. water (adjust as desired)

To create: In advance, peel fresh ripe bananas and freeze until hard. Rehydrate fruit as indicated on page 55. Grind walnuts and flaxseeds to a fine meal using an electric seed grinder.

Pour water into blender and add small chunks of the banana, followed by currants, nuts, seeds and elm powder. Begin blending process. Stop blender at any time ingredients seem to need your assistance. Adjust water as needed and reblend on high speed until smooth and creamy.

Serves 2

Maple Pecan Banana Swirl

What a joy it is when good nourishment tastes like dessert! Be sure to use fresh nuts and pure maple syrup.

2 frozen bananas
¼-⅓ c. fresh pecans
1 T. fresh flaxseed
2 T. maple syrup
2-3 t. slippery elm powder
1 c. water (adjust as needed)

To create: In advance, peel fresh ripe bananas and freeze until hard. Grind pecans and flaxseed using an electric seed grinder. Break bananas into small chunks and combine with water, flax, nuts, sweetener and elm powder in your blender. Blend on high speed until smooth and creamy.

Serves 2

Note: ¼ t. maple flavoring could accent the maple sweetener.

Coconut Crescent Fruit

The ingredients can be varied in this creamy, mineral-rich trio of flavors: banana, date and coconut. Coconut contains organic iodine, a friend to the thyroid. It is soothing to the stomach as well.

2½ frozen bananas
½ c. pitted dates
¼ c. fresh walnuts
¼ c. shredded coconut (opt.)
1 t. lecithin granules
1 c. pure coconut milk
Water and/or soymilk as desired

To create: In advance, peel fresh ripe bananas, and freeze until hard. Soak dates as indicated on page 55. (Some dates, such as Barhi, don't required pre-soaking). Grind walnuts and coconut to a fine meal, using an electric seed grinder. Add coconut milk to your blender, followed by dates, nuts, coconut and small banana chunks. Blend on high speed, adding additional liquid as needed to make drink creamy.

Note: If coconut milk isn't on hand, try using malted vanilla soymilk, along with 1 t. of coconut flavoring. (See section on flavoring essences.)

Serves 2-3

Coconut Lemon Lassie

Do you have some leftover quinoa tucked away in your frig? You won't want to pass up this easy recipe if you do! A blend of nectars transforms the fluffy morsels into a light, vanilla beige-colored delicacy that's rich in energy-giving protein and carbohydrates.

¾ c. quinoa cereal, cooked tender
1-2 T. brown rice syrup
¼-½ t. coconut and lemon flavorings
6 oz. malted vanilla soymilk
½-¾ c. hot water

To create: Have quinoa cereal ready beforehand. Place grains in your blender with sweetener and flavorings. Add hot water and puree smooth, like pudding. Slowly add malted soymilk and continue blending until smooth and silky. Serve warm, or chill for later enjoyment.

Serves 2

Plush Plantain Delight

*Feed your artistic sense of nourishment with this
delectable ethnic combo! It's a rich, earthy, yellow ochre
color, abundant in potassium, vitamin C, and beta
carotene. I like serving it in a unique mug, or
glassware that highlights its originality.*

2 red-skinned bananas (or plantain—about 2 cups)
¼ c. water
1½ t. ghee (clarified butter)
2 t. Sucanat (granulated cane-sugar juice)
1 T. carob molasses syrup
½–1 T. barley malt syrup (or brown rice syrup)
1-2 t. sesame tahini
⅛ t. butterscotch flavoring (I use Frontier brand)
2 c. hot water (adjust)

To create: Peel red bananas or plantain and slice
into rounds (as you would slice a carrot or ordinary
banana). Place fruit in a medium-size, non-stick pan.
Sprinkle with Sucanat before adding water (¼ c.) and
ghee. Sauté fruit over medium-low heat until softened and tender. Transfer to your blender and
combine with sweeteners, flavoring, nut butter and
1 c. cup of the hot water. Blend into a pudding
before adding remaining water. Reblend on high
speed until smooth and creamy. Serve hot or chilled.

Serves 4

Gentle Fig and Mother Grain

Although gentle in its appeal, this delicious, silky-textured drink is a nutritional powerhouse that will provide a body with sustained energy for hours and hours! Served warm, it makes an ideal autumn and winter breakfast or snack! Simply chill for summertime nourishment when the appetite is stifled by heat but needs calories just the same.

4 Calymirna figs, sliced
1 c. boiling water (to rehydrate figs)
1 T. fresh cashew butter or almond butter
¾-1 c. quinoa cereal, cooked tender
1½ T. brown rice syrup
¼ t. vanilla flavoring
6 oz. vanilla malted soymilk
½+ c. water (adjust)

To create: Have quinoa cereal ready beforehand. Slice figs into small pieces. Cover with boiling water and soak until tender. Combine figs (plus soak water), quinoa, cashew butter and sweetener in your blender. Begin blending process. Periodically stop blender to stir ingredients if necessary. When mixture resembles a smooth pudding, slowly add malted soymilk, remaining water (½+ c.) and flavoring. Reblend on high speed until silky and smooth.

Serves 3-4

Peruvian Apple Almond

Quinoa, the wholesome grain whose history begins in Peru, lends this fruit 'n' cereal Smoothie unusual appeal. Imagine yourself borrowing an ancient health custom for your breakfast table. Serve warm or chilled.

½ c. rehydrated apples
½ c. chopped dates
1½-2 c. near-boiling water (to soak fruits)
¾ c. quinoa cereal, cooked tender
4-6 oz. malted almond soymilk

To create: Have quinoa cereal ready beforehand. Pour hot water over dried fruits and let soak until tender. Combine soaked fruit and cereal in your blender. Begin blending process, adding part of the soak water as you go. When the mixture begins to resemble a smooth pudding, add remaining soak water and malted almond milk. Reblend until silky and smooth.

Serves 3-4

Nutty Banana Amaranth

Banana, maple and peanut flavors lend a delicious accent to amaranth, the cereal grain that adds nutritive texture to this Smoothie. The quality of amaranth protein is so good that it exceeds cow's milk in its ability to sustain life!

2 medium-size, frozen bananas
⅓ c. raisins
1 T. smooth peanut butter
1 T. maple syrup
½ c. amaranth cereal (cooked and cooled)
1½+ c. water (adjust)

To create: In advance, peel fresh ripe bananas and freeze until hard. Have cereal ready beforehand. Soak raisins as indicated on page 55. Break frozen banana into small chunks. Puree maple syrup, peanut butter and amaranth with ½ cup water in your blender. Add raisins, bananas and remaining water. Reblend on high speed until smooth.

Serves 3-4

Valencia Spiced Banana

There are so many ways to spice up mellow bananas. Play around with these ingredients and see what you come up with.

1½ frozen bananas
½ c. raw apple, peeled (opt.)
2 t. smooth peanut butter
¼ t. coriander spice
pinch of anise (opt.)
1 T. Sucanat (granular cane-sugar sweetener)
⅔ c. vanilla rice or soy milk
½+ c. water (increase if needed)

To create: In advance, peel fresh, ripe bananas and freeze until hard. Soak raisins as indicated on page 55. Break banana into small pieces and combine with soft raisins, apple, spice, nut butter, sweetener and liquids in your blender. Blend and reblend to achieve a creamy consistency.

Serves 2-4

Banana Sunset

Easy to make with 'leftover' carrot juice.

1½ fresh, ripe bananas, frozen
⅛-¼ c. raisins, soaked
⅔ c. carob soymilk
½ c. carrot juice
pinch cinnamon, optional

To create: In advance, peel fresh bananas and freeze until hard. Soak raisins as indicated on page 55. Break bananas into small chunks and combine in blender with remaining ingredients. Blend smooth.

Sweet Sesame Banana

*High protein nut butters lend a little luxury to this
   Smoothie which is sweet, nourishing and easy to digest.*

1 c. amazake rice milk (original flavor), see p. 103
2 t. fresh almond butter
1 t. sesame tahini
1 large, ripe banana
⅛-¼ c. quinoa cereal, cooked tender (opt.)
1 t. vanilla flavoring
water as needed

To create: If quinoa is desired, have it ready beforehand. Combine amazake, nut butters, sliced banana chunks, flavoring and cereal in your blender. Puree smooth, adding water as needed to achieve the desired consistency.

Serves 1-2

Banana Blossom

It's like ice cream and pudding in one!

1½ fresh, ripe bananas, frozen
½ c. dried apples, soaked
1½ c. apple juice or malted vanilla
soymilk for blending

To create: In advance, peel fresh bananas and freeze until hard. Reconstitute apples as indicated on page 55. Combine fruits with liquid in your blender. Blend on high speed until smooth.

Serves 3.

Soft Banana Barley Nog

This recipe offers a satisfying way to start the body on a cold winter morning. (If you have planned on barley soup for dinner, simmer a pot and set aside some of the cooked morsels for this Smoothie!)

2 medium-size, fresh, ripe bananas, sliced
⅔ c. pearled barley, cooked tender
1 t. almond butter
2 T. rice syrup
1 T. Sucanat
1 t. vanilla flavoring
⅛ t. nutmeg (adjust)
1 c. water
½ c. vanilla soymilk or rice milk (see p. 103)

To create: Heat water on stove top until almost boiling. Combine barley with approximately ½ cup of the hot water in your blender. Puree into a smooth pudding. Stop blender and add banana slices, sweetener, almond butter, flavoring and spice, along with the remaining water. Blend again, slowly adding soymilk or rice milk as needed to make a smooth drink. Sprinkle servings with nutmeg and date sugar.

Serves 4

Frosty Apple Cinnamon Swirl

Commercially prepared Rice Dream is a nutritious
substitute for dairy products in this fruit and nut
enriched taste pleaser. Rice Dream is a frozen dessert,
cream-fashioned from cultured rice, a form of
amazake—see p. 103.

2 c. vanilla Rice Dream (frozen dessert)
⅔ c. rehydrated apples
¼ c. fresh raw pecans
⅛ t. cinnamon powder
2 c. water

To create: Rehydrate dried apples as indicated on page 55. Grind nuts to a fine meal, using an electric seed grinder. Combine softened apples, nuts, spice, Rice Dream and water in your blender. Puree until smooth and creamy.

Serves 2-4

Butterscotch Bliss

Indulge in this Smoothie without guilt! Naturally sweet Rice Dream is fortified with high-protein nuts and healing, slippery elm herb powder.

2 c. vanilla Rice Dream (frozen nondairy dessert)
¼ c. fresh raw pecans
⅛-¼ c. butterscotch chips (or ¼ t. butterscotch flavoring)
2 t. slippery elm powder
1½ c. water (adjust)

To create: Grind fresh nuts to a powdered meal, using an electric seed grinder. Combine with Rice Dream, butterscotch, elm powder and water in your blender. Puree smooth.

Serves 2-4

Golden Apple Almond

The fruit tastes creamy and light in this fiber-rich, golden treat that's easy to make!

2 medium-size, golden-skinned apples, unpeeled
¼ c. golden raisins
1-2 T. shredded coconut flakes (or add ¼ t. coconut flavoring)
¼ c. fresh almonds
2 T. honey
1½ c. water
2-3 ice cubes

To create: Rehydrate raisins as indicated on page 55. Grind coconut and almonds into a fine meal, using an electric seed grinder. Slice apples into small pieces. Combine raisins, apples, nut-meal, honey and water in blender. Blend on high speed until smooth.

Serves 2-3

Crescent Plum

Here's a mellow drink that has the power to gently energize the intestines.

4-5 ripe plums
1½ frozen bananas
1 T. rice syrup
1+ c. apple or pear juice (adjust as desired)
pinch of cinnamon (opt.)

To create: In advance, peel fresh, ripe bananas and freeze until hard. Lightly peel plums and slice. Combine with juice, sweetener, banana and spice in the blender. Puree until smooth.

Serves 2

Almond Pear and Date

Make this sweet, nourishing nectar when you have some almond nutmilk on hand and enjoy a hefty sip of minerals.

2½-3 c. almond nutmilk
3 ripe pears (such as Bartlett or Comice)
¼ c. dates
⅛ c. fresh raw almonds (opt.)
¼-½ t. cinnamon powder
½-1 t. vanilla flavoring (opt.)

To create: See *Liquids Giving Luster* (page 95) for instructions on preparing nutmilk. Rehydrate dates. Grind almonds, using an electric seed grinder. Peel pears and slice into blender. Add nutmilk, soft dates, cinnamon, nuts, nutmilk and flavoring if desired. Blend until smooth.

Serves 4

Variations on Pear: You could substitute dates with soaked raisins and orange flavoring could replace vanilla.

Gingery Autumn Butterfruit

Sweet, ripe, buttery pears are gently spiced in this drink,
which could be served warm, alongside a muffin.

3-4 ripe pears (such as red Bartlett or Comice)
2+ T. maple syrup
1 T. rice syrup
1 t. light molasses (opt.)
½ c. malted vanilla soymilk (or almond)
2+ c. water (adjust)
¼ t. ginger
½ t. cinnamon
⅛ t. cloves (powder)
⅛ t. almond flavoring (opt.)

To create: Peel and slice pears into your blender. Add sweeteners, spices and liquids. Blenderize smooth. Drink immediately.

Serves 3-4

Note: Omit almond flavoring if using almond milk. Almond milk, versus vanilla, will produce a darker-colored drink.

Ginger Mint Pear

Pears, ginger spice and mint offer soothing refreshment to the stomach and digestive tract.

3 ripe pears (such as Bartlett or Comice)
½ t. fresh ginger grated (or ¼ t. ginger powder to taste)
⅛-¼ t. mint extract
1-2 T. honey
½-1 c. Rice Dream (frozen dessert)
½ c. water (adjust as needed)
½ c. sparkling water (opt.)

To create: Peel pears and slice into your blender. Add ginger, mint, sweetener and Rice Dream. Adjust water as needed to blend smooth. Taste, and add sparkling water if desired. Drink immediately.

Serves 3-4

Tutti Fruit Tang

Reach into your fruit bowl for nature's most popular tree-grown snacks and blend into a satisfying sip.

1 ripe banana
1 golden apple
1 ripe pear
2 T. golden raisins
1 c. orange juice (adjust)

To create: Rehydrate raisins as indicated on page 55. Peel banana and lightly peel apple and pear. Combine all fruits in the blender with juice and puree until smooth.

Serves 2

Rhubarb and Raisin Spice

Potassium, calcium, iron and fiber are some of the hidden benefits in this tangy fruit blend.

½ c. frozen rhubarb chunks (sold in frozen food section at grocery store)
2 medium-size apples
¾ c. golden raisins
2 T. honey (adjust as desired)
½+ c. apple juice
½ c. vanilla malted soymilk (opt.)
⅛-¼ t. ginger and cinnamon
⅛-¼ t. lemon flavoring (opt.)

To create: Rehydrate raisins as indicated on page 55. Lightly peel apples and slice into small pieces. Combine frozen rhubarb, apples, soft raisins, sweetener, spices and liquid in your blender. Blend on high speed until smooth.

Serves 3

Variation: For variation on this drink, you could stew rhubarb slightly and increase the amount used. Raw apples could be substituted with rehydrated dried apples. And you could serve it warm instead of chilled.

Smoothies in Earth Tones
of Green and Blue

Avocado Apple Carrot Jewel

Here's a sip of "light protein" that tastes refreshing and
gives instant energy!

1 medium-large, fresh, ripe avocado, pitted
1 c. fresh pineapple
1 c. apple juice (adjust)
½ c. carrot juice
1 t. spirulina powder (opt.)

To create: Peel and slice avocado and pineapple
into small chunks. Combine with fresh juices and
green algae powder (spirulina) in blender and puree
smooth.

Serves 2

Avocado Pineapple Paradise

This light, frothy Smoothie is a "clean, green," luminous
color that impresses tastebuds every time. Serve with a
wedge of lime, in pretty glass tumblers.

1 medium-large, fresh, ripe avocado, pitted
1½ c. fresh pineapple
1 T. honey or rice syrup
1½ c. orange juice
2 t. lime juice (opt.)
¼ t. coconut flavoring
2 ice cubes

To create: Peel and slice avocado and pineapple
into small chunks. Combine with sweetener, flavorings and juices in blender. Puree smooth. Add ice
cubes, if desired, and reblend.

Serves 2

Mocha Mint Avocado Whip

Although this Smoothie is a classy tint of brown, it features fresh green avocado fruit. Perhaps its delicious, nutritious taste is all that really matters!

1 medium large, fresh ripe avocado (pitted)
1½ c. vanilla frozen amazake (see p. 103)
3-4 t. Cafix (roasted cereal-grain powder)
1 T. honey
¼-½ t. mint flavoring
½-¾ c. water

To create: Peel and slice avocado into chunks. Combine with frozen amazake, Cafix, sweetener, flavoring and water in the blender. Puree smooth. Serve in sleek tumblers.

Serves 2-4

Pineapple Ocean

This is a cinch to make if you have these no-fuss ingredients on hand.

1½ c. pure coconut milk (½ c. apple juice could replace part of coconut milk)
2 c. pineapple chunks
1-2 t. spirulina powder (opt.)

To create: Peel and slice pineapple into small chunks. Combine with coconut milk and spirulina in the blender and puree smooth.

Serves 2

Kiwi Fruit Cocktail

*On a hot summer day, this is a tangy and refreshing,
  electrolytic thirst quencher.*

3 fresh, ripe kiwi fruit
1 frozen banana
1 c. apple juice
2 c. coconut-fruit juice blend
strawberry garnish

To create: In advance, peel fresh, ripe banana and
freeze until hard. Peel and slice kiwi fruit. Break
banana into small chunks. Combine kiwi, banana
and juices in blender. Puree smooth. Garnish servings with a fresh strawberry.

Serves 3-4

Note: I used Summer Song brand coconut-fruit
juice which blends coconut with white grape juice.
2 T. aloe vera juice could also be blended into this
drink, but you may choose to omit the banana if you
add it.

Earthy Herb and Veggie

This flavorful drink offers earthy nourishment.
The pea-green color might remind you of soup,
so why not serve it in a little cup with an accent
of celery leaf, cherry tomato and a sesame cracker?

2½-3 c. tomato juice, chilled
¼-⅓ c. soft tofu
¼ c. corn
2 T. spinach leaves
⅓ c. salad greens (Romaine, parsley, cubes, etc.)
1-2 t. fresh lovage leaf
Spike (herbal seasoner) to taste
1 T. Bragg's amino bouillon (opt.)
2 ice cubes

To create: Combine tomato juice, tofu, corn, green and herb seasoners in the blender. Puree smooth. Add ice cubes and reblend.

Serves 2

Blueberry Lemon Bliss

*Silky in texture, this purplish-blue nectar is soothing to
the digestive system and offers light nourishment to the
whole body.*

1½-2 c. dairy-free tapioca, cooked and chilled
1+ c. frozen blueberries
1 T. honey or maple syrup (adjust)
¼ t. lemon flavoring
½-1 c. water or coconut milk (adjust)
3 ice cubes

To create: In advance, prepare tapioca as indicated
on page 74. Combine with blueberries, honey, lemon
and liquid in your blender. Puree smooth. Adjust
liquids with precision to create a silky versus
slippery texture.

Serves 3

Blueberry Tofu Almond

Blueberries and maple syrup go hand in hand in this drink that's delicious for breakfast or quick replenishment after exercise.

1½ c. blueberries (fresh or frozen)
1 frozen banana
¼ c. soft tofu (opt.)
2 T. maple syrup
¼ t. almond flavoring
1+ c. water or coconut milk

To create: In advance, peel banana and freeze until hard. Combine with blueberries, tofu, sweetener, flavoring and water in your blender. Puree smooth.

Serves 2

Blueberry Apple Blossom

Soothing and calming in its appeal, blue is a fun color to drink!

2+ c. apple juice (adjust)
1½ c. blueberries
1 c. rehydrated apples
1-2 T. honey
⅛ t. cinnamon to taste
¼ c. fresh raw almonds
⅛ t. coconut flavoring (opt.)

To create: Rehydrate apples as indicated on page 55. Grind almonds to a fine meal, using an electric seed grinder. Combine soft apples, blueberries, honey, cinnamon, nuts and juice in blender. Puree smooth.

Serves 2-3

Smoothies in Earth Tones
of Brown and Purple

Pearly Prune 'n' Sesame

Sweet prunes (dried plums) blend perfectly with hearty barley and mellow sweeteners in this creamy, brown Smoothie that is excellent for increasing vitality and blood circulation.

½ c. rehydrated prunes (plus ½ c. soak water)
1 frozen banana
½-¾ c. pearled barley (cooked)
2 t. sesame tahini
2 T. Sucanat
1 T. brown rice syrup
1¾ c. water (adjust)

To create: In advance, peel ripe banana and freeze until hard. Have barley ready beforehand. Slice prunes and rehydrate as indicated on page 55. Break banana into small segments. Add barley, tahini, sweeteners and approximately ¾+ c. water to your blender. Puree into a smooth pudding. Add soft prunes, banana pieces and remaining water to your blender. Begin blending process. Stop blender to stir ingredients, if needed. Continue to blend until smooth. Serve warm or chilled.

Serves 4

Roasted Carob Mint Barley

This sweet, hearty grain drink, made delicious by accents
of roasted grain powder and carob, is rich in minerals
and calcium. Barley nourishes body weight in a
beautiful way!

⅔-1 c. pearled barley (cooked)
1 T. Cafix powder
1½ T. carob powder
½ t. cocoa powder
1-2 T. honey
dash of barley malt sweetener
¼ c. fresh, raw almonds or walnuts
⅛ t. mint flavoring
1+ c. hot water (adjust)
½ c. vanilla soymilk

To create: Have barley ready beforehand. Combine barley with approximately ¾-1 c. of the water in your blender. Puree into a smooth pudding (adjusting water as needed). Add Cafix, carob, cocoa, sweeteners, mint flavoring and soymilk. Blend mixture again. If nuts are desired, grind them to a fine meal using an electric seed grinder and reblend until smooth.

Serves 3

Raisin Spice Sweet Potato

*If you like raisins you'll really enjoy them in this anise
and orange-spiced drink that is made creamy by the
addition of sweet potatoes. Its nutritional value can't
be beat!*

1-1¼ c. dark raisins
2 medium-size sweet potatoes
2 T. Sucanat
1 T. maple syrup
¼-½ t. anise powder
⅛ t. lemon flavoring (opt.)
⅓ c. orange juice
1½-2 c. water (adjust)

To create: In advance, bake sweet potatoes until
tender as indicated on page 67. (Let cool in the
refrigerator.) Rehydrate raisins as indicated on page
55. Peel skins from potatoes and slice into small
chunks. Puree soaked raisins with the orange juice
(plus a bit more water if needed). When raisins
become smooth in texture, add sweeteners, flavorings and spices and continue blending. Add sweet
potatoes and remaining water. Stop blender at any
time to stir ingredients. Reblend until smooth and
creamy. Serve warm or chilled.

Serves 3-4

Frosty Banana Carob Chip

*Everyone from kids to adults loves this creamy treat.
Carob chips lend it a soft, speckled color.*

2 medium-size, frozen bananas
1 c. vanilla frozen amazake (see p. 103)
1 T. unsalted peanut butter
¼+ c. carob chips
1-2 t. slippery elm powder
¾-1 c. water

To create: Ahead of time, peel ripe bananas and freeze until hard. Break bananas into small segments and combine in your blender with frozen amazake, nut butter, carob chips, elm powder and water. Puree smooth.

Serves 2-4

Tahini Banana

Here's a "soft-as-velvet" sip of flavor.

2 frozen bananas
2 c. carob soymilk (adjust)
1-2 t. sesame tahini
2 t. carob molasses syrup (opt.)

To create: Ahead of time, peel ripe bananas and freeze until hard. Break bananas into small segments and combine in your blender with sesame tahini, syrup and soymilk.

Serves 2

Silk Chocolate Sweet Potato

Cocoa-spiced sweet potatoes are irresistible in this creamy, brown drink that tastes like pudding! Call your friends and kids in for a sip. They'll never guess how nutritious it is!

2 medium-large sweet potatoes (about 2½ c.)
1 T. unsalted peanut butter (or fresh cashew butter)
2+ T. maple syrup
2 T. cocoa powder
1½ t. vanilla flavoring
1½-2 c. hot water (adjust); ½ c. malted vanilla soymilk could replace part of water

To create: In advance, bake sweet potatoes until tender, as indicated on page 67. Let cool in refrigerator. Peel skins from potatoes and slice in small chunks. Add hot water to blender; follow by nut butter, sweetener, cocoa, soymilk, flavoring and sweet potatoes. Begin blending process. Stop blender at any time to stir ingredients. Reblend until smooth

Serves 3-4

Variation: Substitute cocoa powder with 1½ T. carob powder. Add 1+ c. water and ½ c. malted vanilla soymilk.

Sesame Carob Yam

*This Smoothie offers a variation on "Silk Chocolate
Sweet Potato." It can be fortified with sesame tahini
and quinoa.*

2 medium-size sweet potatoes (about 2 c.)
2 T. carob powder
2-3 t. cocoa powder
1 T. sesame tahini
2-3 T. maple syrup
1 t. vanilla flavoring
2-3 T. quinoa cereal, cooked (opt.)
2-2½ c. hot water

To create: In advance, bake sweet potatoes until
tender, as indicated on page 67. Let cool in
refrigerator. Peel skins from potatoes and slice in
small chunks. Pour 1½ c. of water into your blender.
Add sweet potatoes, carob, cocoa, tahini, syrup and
flavoring. Add remaining water and begin blending
process. Stop blender at any time to stir ingredients
if needed. Resume blending process. Puree until
smooth and creamy. Quinoa may be added last if
desired.

Serves 2-4

Maple Morning Teff

Iron, calcium, potassium and nutrient-rich bran are but a few of the nutriments you'll gain from this tasty fruit, nut and cereal, textured drink.

½ c. teff cereal (cooked)
¼ c. rehydrated raisins
1½ frozen bananas (or fresh)
2 T. fresh, raw almonds (ground to meal)
1 t. almond butter
1-2 T. maple syrup
1 t. vanilla flavoring (opt.)
1½-2 c. water (adjust)

To create: In advance, peel fresh, ripe bananas and freeze until hard. Have teff ready beforehand. Rehydrate raisins as indicated on page 55. Break bananas into small segments. Combine bananas, raisins, nut butters, sweetener, flavoring and water in your blender. Begin blending process. Stop blender at any time to stir ingredients. Add teff last and blend on high speed until smooth. (Adjust water as needed.)

Variation: Substitute almond butter with 1 T. peanut butter. Replace vanilla flavoring with coconut flavoring. Sweeten with carob molasses syrup. Blend with Amazake rice milk or malted vanilla soymilk.

Serves 3+

Carob Teff Treat

Teff, almonds and carob chips add nourishing texture to this frosty treat.

½ c. teff cereal (cooked)
2 c. nondairy ice cream
(Try swiss almond, vanilla or carob mint.)
¼ c. carob chips
⅛ c. fresh raw almonds

To create: Have teff ready beforehand. Grind fresh almonds to a fine meal using an electric seed grinder. Combine teff, almonds, carob chips and nondairy ice cream in your blender. Puree smooth.

Serves 2

Grapevine Cooler

Here's the kind of nourishment that's easy to prepare and easier to swallow!

2 frozen bananas
2 c. grape juice (adjust)
1-2 T. flaxseed (opt.)

To create: ahead of time, peel ripe bananas and freeze until hard. Break bananas into small segments and combine in your blender with grape juice. Grind flaxseed, using an electric seed grinder and add, if desired, before blending Smoothie.

Serves 2

Directory of Sources: Super Smoothie Ingredients

Most natural food cooperatives and health food stores stock the ingredients found in Super Smoothies recipes. The following distributors supply those retailers. Their mail order catalogs are available for your convenience and you may order certain items directly from the company itself if necessary.

Nuts, Seeds and Dried Fruit

Jaffe Bros.
28560 Hilac Road
P.O. Box 636
Valley Center, CA 92080
(617) 749-1133
Mail order; dried fruits, oils, nuts, seeds, carob powder, etc.

Walnut Acres
Penns Creek, PA 17862
(717) 837-0601
Mail order, high quality; no preservatives, rain forest nuts, organic sunflower seeds and preserves.

Erewhon, Inc.
236 Washington Street
Brookline, MA 02146
(800) 222-8028
Mail order; nuts and nut butters, seeds, etc.

K. B. Hall Ranch
11999 Ojai S. P. Road
Ojai, CA 93025
(805) 646-4512
Mail order; preservative-free dried apricots and walnuts.

International Protein Industries, Inc.
P. O. Box 871
Smithtown, NY 11787
Chemical-free hulled sesame seeds.

Norganic Foods Co.
163 E. Liberty Avenue
Anaheim, CA 92801
(714) 870-9820
Dried fruits.

Ahlers Organic Date and Grapefruit Garden
P. O. Box 726
Mecca, CA 92254
(610) 396-2337
Mail order; organically-grown dates.

Flaxseed

Arrowhead Mills
P. O. Box 866
Hereford, TX 79045
(806) 364-0730
Organically-grown flaxseed; whole, unground.

Omega Life, Inc.
15355 Woodbridge Road
Brookfield, WI 53005
(414) 786-2070
Flaxseed ground to powder and combined with nutritional co-factors.

Fruitful Yield
4950 W. Oakton
Skokie, IL
(312) 679-8975
Features gaurgum (a substitute for flaxseed, if desired).

Flavoring Extracts

Cook Flavoring Co.
Cook's Choice Extracts
P. O. Box 890
Tacoma, WA 98401
(206) 627-5499
Mail order; retail flavoring extracts in a high-quality array of flavors.

Frontier Cooperative Herbs
Box 69
Norway, Iowa 53218
Twenty-five natural flavors, all natural, no alcohol or preservatives.

Natural Sweeteners

Lundberg Farms
Richvale, CA 95974-0369
Organic brown rice syrup.

Spring Tree Corporation
P. O. Box 1160
Brattleboro, VT 05301
(802) 254-8784
Organic maple syrup, carob powder.

Horizon Natural Products
Soquel, CA
Stevia Sweet Leaf Powder.

Now Foods
Villa Park, IL 60181
Stevia Sweet Leaf Powder.

Bronner's Sweeteners
P. O. Box 28
Escondido, CA 92025
(619) 745-7069; 743-2211
Dr. Bronner's Barley Malt and Calcium Malt Powder.

Juices and Fruit Preserves

Sorrell Ridge Farm
100 Markley Street
Port Reading, NJ 07064
(201) 636-2060
Fruit conserves.

Norganic Foods Co.
163 E. Liberty Avenue
Anaheim, CA 92801
(714) 870-1820
Fruit conserves.

Fruit conserves.

Heinke's
5365 Clark Road
Paradise, CA 95969-6399
(916) 877-4847
Features fresh fruit juices with no sweeteners added.

Non-Dairy Milk

Grainaissance, Inc.
1580 62nd Street
Emeryville, CA 94608
Sweet Rice Milk (Amazake).

Epicurean International
P. O. Box 13242
Berkeley, CA 94701
Pure coconut milk.

Non-Toxic Cleaners

Nutri-Biotic Systems
Lakeport, CA 95453
(707) 263-0411
Liquid concentrate for cleaning fruits and vegetables.

Special Extras

Red Saffron Herbs
3009 16th Avenue South
Minneapolis, MN 55407
Features bee pollen, spices and Slippery Elm Powder.

American Health Products
El Molino Foods
Ramsey, NJ 07446
Carob powder.

Super Blue-Green Algae Products
P.O. Box 802
Willernie, MN 55090
(800) 927-2527, ext. 5378

Into the Spirit of
Sport and Fitness

If getting into the flow of fitness sometimes means arriving at a place other than your neighborhood gym or fitness center, why not rediscover nature's playground?

It's open every day and season of your life and always offers to invigorate you with free-spirited energy.

And what a way it has, of pleasantly distracting the ego from its proud attachment to the body. Amidst nature's awesome presence it's so natural to feel beauty and empowerment from within.

To also notice how all the things in nature are stimulated through a process of growth and eternal renewal, is to awaken the same power within ourselves!

So, then, when you step outdoors into the scenery which brings this fresh and colorful awareness to life, let its infinite magnitude and creativity inspire your transformation, strength and longevity!

Meditation
on the Move

(An outdoor exercise for integrating body, mind and spirit.)

Inhale the outdoor air as if to re-experience your first breaths for life. Let the wonders of the cosmos revive the spark of your aliveness in the world.

Salute the radiant sun and draw its warmth into yourself. Remember that its golden light dwells within you, offering to keep your heart open, your awareness bright.

Find trees to embrace. Lean on them openly as if they were old friends. Accept their wisdom for stretching your tendons and muscles they way their own roots and branches do.

Take to new pathways that will welcome your bike, skis, skates and sporting shoes. Connect the soles (souls) of your feet not to the hard pavement, but to the soft ear of a Mother Earth who listens for the rhythm of our attunement.

Set any sails you own to the music that plays freely in the wind, and swim in synchronicity with the creative fluids of your being.

Bend and flex a barbell while reaching for an open sky. Bring down a sense of the almighty, yet dismiss not the vigor in a tiny bird that flies.

Listen to, see, and feel every vein of life which co-exists. Mingle its natural beauty with your own and be transfused with gratitude.

Let your gratitude turn to love, and let your love become the nectar that nourishes you. You are as powerful and unique as your Creator honorably blessed you.